Enticing International Recipes from Latin America

Enticing International Recipes from Latin America

Vilma Janke Grace

Published by **ACROPOLIS BOOKS Ltd.** • Washington D.C. 20009

ACROPOLIS BOOKS LTD.
Colortone Building, 2400 17th St., N.W.
Washington, D.C. 20009

Printed in the United States of America by
COLORTONE PRESS, Creative Graphics Inc.
Washington, D.C. 20009

ACROPOLIS BOOKS
are distributed in

EUROPE AND THE BRITISH COMMONWEALTH
by Paul Maitland, 2/16 Mount Sion,
Tunbridge Wells, Kent TN1 1UF, England

Designs appearing in this book are from
DESIGN MOTIFS OF ANCIENT MEXICO and
DESIGNS FROM PRE-COLUMBIA MEXICO,
both by Jorge Enciso, Dover Publications, Inc. New York
Drawings appearing in this cookbook are by the author.
Cover photo courtesy Américas Monthly Magazine published
by the General Secretariat of the Organization of American States.

Library of Congress Cataloging in Publication Data

Grace, Vilma Janke
LATIN AMERICAN & Cholesterol Conscious COOKING

Includes index.
1. Cookery, International. 2. Low-cholesterol diet--Recipes. I. Title.
TX725.A1G67 641.5'63 79-15727
ISBN 0-87491-280-6

Acknowledgments

To gather data for this book our family ate at many restaurants in Latin America. We found a great variety of intriguing native, Chinese, Italian, French, and international restaurants. We shared our experiences and togetherness as a family during these meals while experimenting with new dishes.

My special thanks go to my husband Bob, who encouraged me to start this cookbook, and to our five children, who shared this great gourmet adventure with us.

Vilma J. Grace

Foreword

My interest in cooking started when we moved from the United States to Puerto Rico. The aroma emanating from the neighboring homes with their open kitchen windows was enough to get me started on the road to new kitchen experiences. During our further travels in Central and South America, we tried even wider varieties of native foods. In Lima, Peru, we visited many restaurants and tried their menus. Some of the dishes had a touch of hot pepper while others were so strong they would set your tongue on fire.

In Lima, we visited the famous "Chifas," well known for their Chinese dishes. Here, I began to take an interest in Chinese cooking. When we were in Panama, I enrolled in a Chinese cooking class. The classes were an experience not easily forgotten. We would arrive at the cooking class before lunch time and our teacher would prepare simple oriental dishes. We learned how to fix and cook them ourselves, sampling each other's attempts.

When we left Panama and moved to Brazil, a whole new gastronomical experience opened up for us in Rio de Janeiro. We ate at many restaurants in Copacabana. These were varied enough to satisfy the connoisseur of good cuisine.

All these recipes were tried in our kitchen, with the assistance of local residents and professional cooks with their own special talents. In this cookbook, I have tried to present the best dishes, based on our travels in Latin America. The fat content of all these recipes has been considered, aiming at making meals relatively low in cholesterol. Cholesterol is a fatty substance present in foods of animal origin, and should be avoided.

As a mother of five I was concerned about the high cholesterol in our family's diet but desired to continue providing my family with the foods we so dearly loved. Reviewing my recipes with an eye on cholesterol and fat content I found that these substances could largely be eliminated while still keeping the basic character and flavor of the original recipe. Here, then, is my collection of favorite recipes, reviewed and modified for cholesterol conscious cooking.

I hope the reader enjoys these appetizing recipes as much as we have.

Introduction

A Heart Surgeon Looks At Cholesterol

As a heart surgeon I cannot emphasize enough the importance of a low saturated fat and low cholesterol diet to fight arteriosclerotic disease which affects so severely millions of people in this country. Follow-up analysis in the recovery and rehabilitation of many heart surgery patients reveals that most of them who follow a careful diet along with other important practices such as not smoking, daily exercise and weight reduction programs do well and re-adjust to normal life.

The level of circulating cholesterol in the blood is a major indicator of risk, a fact confirmed by epidemiologic studies of the past four decades. Diets containing cholesterol above 300 milligrams per day appear to elevate the cholesterol level in the blood. And, since the average American diet contains from 600 milligrams to 1 gram of cholesterol per day, restriction in cholesterol content to 300 milligrams per day, as well as a diet low in saturated fats can prove very beneficial.

In this book Vilma Janke Grace puts together very palatable modified dishes from different countries which will enhance the acceptance of these diet principles. I wish her success in this praiseworthy endeavor.

Ruben Ungaro M.D.
Cardiovascular and Thoracic Surgeon

Contents

Seven Fiesta Menus

LATIN AMERICAN BRUNCH

Decorate table with whole green and red cabbages, into which small cubes of cheeses, and black and green stuffed olives are stuck with toothpicks. Place rose radishes all around green cabbage and leaf lettuce around red cabbage.

Dominican Fried Sticks Cassava 19
Fiesta Rolls 23
Savory Omelets 78
Spinach-Cheese & Pork Souffle 72
Meringues 101
Beverage 105

CARNIVAL NIGHT

Decorate table with a large basket filled with luscious tropical fruit, i.e., pineapple, oranges, mangoes, avocados, bananas, etc.

Carnival Bean Salad 30
Fillet of Flounder and Shrimp from Bahia 43
Rice 85
Caribbean Fruit Salad 104
Beverage 105

VIVA LA JARANA NIGHT!

Surround fish with leaf lettuce, small slices of cooked corn on the cob, as well as small cooked slices of sweet potato.

Marinated Fish 21
Pepper Chicken and Walnuts 64
Rice 85
Mixed Green Salad 31
Caramel Bananas 101
Beverage 105

CARIBBEAN NIGHT

Use lots of fruit as a center piece!

Peruvian Shish Kebabs 52
Chicken with Rice #2 63
Avocado Salad 29
Caramel Custard 91
Beverage 105

GAUCHO NIGHT

Marinated Carrots (with lots of olives around carrots) 20
Stuffed Flank Steak (leaf lettuce all around) 60
Escalloped Potatoes 87
Creole Green Beans 88
Cream Puffs 92
Beverage 105

LOS ANDES NIGHT

Place a tomato rose in the center of pancakes as a decoration. To make a tomato rose, peel tomato, keeping the skin in a long strip, and arrange peel like a beautiful rose.

Corn Pancakes 89
Tuna Fish Salad with Walnuts 32
Colombian Style Chicken 70
Rice 85
Molded Cold Peach Cake 99
Beverage 105

SOUTH OF THE BORDER LUNCHEON

Decorate with lots of fresh fruit and flowers.

Stuffed Avocados with Chicken 81
Argentinian Beef Stew 54
Rice 85
Filled Cookies 96
Beverage 105

Let's Talk About Cholesterol

Most researchers agree that cholesterol is somehow associated with heart disease, as are other risk factors such as obesity and hypertension. Many nutritionists believe that changes in the American diet have contributed to the dramatic increase in heart disease in this country, especially the greater consumption of calories as saturated fat and cholesterol. Therefore they recommended reducing the amount of saturated animal products such as hard cheeses, whole milk, butter, and eggs in the diet. Chicken and fish are lower in cholesterol than red meat; organ meats and seafood such as shrimp, lobster, sardines, crabs and clams tend to be higher and should be eaten only occasionally.

The recipes in this book were chosen not only for gourmet appeal but also to aid those individuals who are cholesterol-conscious and would like to prepare delicious foods while making recommended dietary changes. Egg yolks contain the single highest concentration of cholesterol. For this reason, recipes using eggs contain the minimum amount of egg which will still result in an optimal product.

Hints to Reduce Fat & Cholesterol in Food

Bread	When a bread recipe calls for shortening, margarine or butter, use vegetable oil. It's best to use unbleached flour instead of all purpose flour which has lost its nutritional value in the bleaching process.
Grease	To dispose of grease in soups, gravies, etc. very quickly add a whole tray of ice cubes to the liquid and the grease will cling to the cubes. Throw cubes with grease away. Or, if you are not in a big hurry, place liquid in refrigerator overnight. Grease will harden and can then be thrown away.
Margarine	When you buy margarine, make sure that the first ingredient on the label is listed as liquid vegetable oil.
Milk	You can keep your cholesterol intake low by using low fat and skim milk products. When a recipe calls for milk, remember that by mixing 1/3 cup nonfat powdered milk with 2/3 cup water, you are eliminating the fat content of the milk. Also, you will be realizing quite a saving, since the price of milk has gone up sharply. Always buy evaporated skimmed milk instead of the regular evaporated milk.
Saturated fats	These are usually solid at room temperature, like butter, cheese and lard. These will raise the blood cholesterol level.
Olive Oil	This oil does not affect blood cholesterol.
Vegetable Oils	Always use polyunsaturated vegetable oil! Vegetable oil contains linoleic acid, which is absolutely necessary for our body to grow lean and healthy. Linoleic acid must be supplied by what we eat. One tablespoon daily of almost any vegetable oil in our diet will prevent a deficiency in linoleic acid. Always use liquid vegetable oils for cooking, not butter or margarine. Corn oil, safflower oil and soy bean oil are the most unsaturated and the best to use.
Mayonnaise	Imitation mayonnaise, though less tasty, can be substituted to cut down on the fat and cholesterol in regular mayonnaise.

Garnishes

A garnish is placed on a serving dish to make the food more appealing. It is not desirable to garnish too many dishes at any meal. An appropriate garnish should be applied to the main dish, leaving the rest of the dishes plain, except for salads, which can look very colorful with the right garnishes. The garnish should always be the right size in relation to the food,–not too big with a small dish and not too small on a large platter of food. A garnish should be placed wherever it looks best on the plate, usually in an empty space.

Commonly used garnishes include parsley, watercress, romaine or loose-leaf lettuce, curly endive, hard boiled eggs, olives, radishes, paprika, clusters of grapes, sliced cucumbers, orange rind, etc. . . .

Pies may be self-garnished by shaping the edge of the crust with a finger or the handle of a knife. Icing and frosting can be spread on a cake in so many different ways. You can create graceful swirl effects by spreading frosting with a spoon.

The purpose of using garnishes is to make the food you serve more attractive to the eye. Put your artistic ideas to work in choosing the right type of garnish and arranging it attractively.

Hints to Save Money

Bean Sprouts	Sprout your own. It's lots of fun! Place 1 cup of Soy beans inside a clean empty 1 gallon (i.e. milk) plastic container, with the top part cut off, leaving the handle on the container. Fill it with water and soak beans overnight, about 10 hours. Pour off water. Place container on its side until beans sprout. Keep moist at all times, by pouring lukewarm water over the beans twice a day. Always make sure you drain them well. Beans should be kept damp, not wet. When sprouts are ready (it will take about 6 days for beans to sprout), wash and remove skins and hairlike ends. Use in your favorite recipe. Yields about 3½ cups of sprouts.
Fish	Fish fillets are much cheaper by the pound if you buy the fish whole and tell the person in charge of the seafood department to fillet it, save the bones and also clean the head (these items which are usually discarded, make a very nutritious fish stock). Sea trout and mackerel are usually good buys when in season.
Eggs	Since you will be using more egg whites than egg yolks in some of the recipes, don't throw the left over yolks away. Save them. You can place 1 or 2 egg yolks in a blender with 1/3 cup olive oil and the juice of 1/2 lemon. Blend 30 seconds and use as a hair conditioner. Rub this mixture all over hair. Leave it on for 1 hour. Shampoo and rinse your hair as usual. You will have a very healthy head of hair!
Ginger Root	Buy one fresh ginger root. Slice it very fine and place in the blender with 1/2 cup vegetable oil and 1 teaspoon salt. Blend for 30 seconds. Place this creamy mixture in a covered jar and freeze. This method will preserve the ginger without the stringy condition which becomes apparent when it's kept too long.
Pork	Buy a very large pork loin roast (a better cut than a pork rib end roast). You can then have butcher slice only as much as you need for pork chops and you can bake the rest in a 350° oven for 2 hours (usually 40 minutes per lb.) and prepare your favorite pork recipe. There is no extra charge for this service.)

Pressure Cooking	I find this method of cooking very economical in saving time and energy. When a recipe calls for a long period of cooking time, use your pressure cooker and dinner will be ready in no time at all. In some cases, this is much faster than if you used a microwave oven. Never leave your pressure cooker unattended or at high heat. High internal pressure will cause the valve to blow up and you will end up with food liquid all over your kitchen ceiling and lots of things to clean up!
Rice	Make large amounts of rice. Usually, four cups of uncooked rice will make enough for 3 or 4 rice recipes for a family of 6. Cooked rice will keep in refrigerator in a covered container for approximately one week. Use as needed for preparing chinese fried rice dishes, or simply re-heat by placing in a pan with 1/4 cup water, cover and place over medium heat for 5 minutes. Also, if you add a few drops of lemon juice to the cooking water of uncooked rice it will be more grainy in appearance.
Salad Dressing	There's no need to buy salad dressing at the supermarket. It not only contains preservatives, but also is expensive. Make your own by following my instructions inside this cookbook. If kept in a well covered jar in the refrigerator, it will stay fresh for many months, but if you like to eat salads like we do in our family, your salad dressing won't last long!
Spaghetti Sauce	Sweeten sauce with a ripe apple which has been washed, cored, sliced and placed in a blender with 1 cup burgundy wine. You can also sweeten it with a large carrot, which has been scraped and sliced thinly, then put in the blender with the wine and 1 or 2 teaspoons of honey. This will eliminate using sugar to sweeten the sauce. Sometimes, I have even added 1/2 cup of fresh or frozen orange juice to the sauce, and the result was as tasty as it could be!
Steaks	When buying beef for steaks, the best way to get the most for your money is to pick a good size rib roast and have the butcher cut it to desired thickness. This will save you quite a bit of money per pound *and* there is no extra charge for this service.

Recipes

Appetizers

YUCA FRITA DOMINICANA

Dominican Fried Cassava Sticks

These are very tasty.

1-1/2 lb frozen Cassava root
(sold in Latin markets)
4 cups water
1/3 cup veg oil
Salt, to taste

Place frozen cassava pieces in pan with water. Let it come to a boil. Cover and cook over medium heat for 35 minutes, or until well done. Drain well.

When cool enough, slice cassava like thick french fries.

In large frying pan, heat oil; in it fry cassava sticks till crisp and a light golden color.

Place cassava on paper towels and sprinkle sticks with salt.

Serve hot. About 2 dozen cassava sticks.

GARBANZOS SALTADOS

Garbanzo Nuts

Chick peas are good at cocktail time! Bolivia

1 lb canned chick peas
1/2 cup veg oil
1/2 tsp salt
1/4 tsp Cayenne pepper
1/4 tsp garlic powder

Drain chick peas well. Dry with paper towels.

Place in 300° oven to dry for half an hour.

In large skillet, heat oil; in it saute chick peas, turning frequently, until they turn gold and crisp.

Place on paper towels, sprinkle with salt, Cayenne pepper and garlic powder.

Serve hot as hors d'oeuvre. Serves 4.

ZANAHORIAS ENCURTIDAS

Marinated Carrots

These are great when company is coming and very well liked in Paraguay.

5 med size carrots
3 tbsp veg oil
3 cloves garlic, chopped
1 tbsp onion, chopped
1/4 cup cider vinegar
1-1/2 tsp salt
1/2 tsp mustard
1 tsp dried basil
1/8 tsp pepper
1/4 tsp Cayenne pepper
1 onion, thinly sliced

Scrape carrots, rinse and cut into three inch strips.

In large skillet, heat oil; in it saute garlic and chopped onion, until tender, about 5 minutes.

Stir in vinegar, salt, mustard, basil, pepper and carrots. Simmer, covered, 5 minutes. Carrots should still be crunchy and crisp.

Transfer carrot mixture to shallow dish. Top with layer of sliced onions, Cayenne pepper. Cover.

Refrigerate, basting occasionally. Serves 5.

RIO BLANCO

Onion Rings

Peru. One of our most cherished recipes (given to the author by her father). These will stay crisp.

1 cup flour
1 tbsp baking powder
2/3 cup water
Vegetable oil for frying
3 large onions, peeled and sliced 1/4 inch thick
Salt

Mix flour, baking powder and water.

In large heavy skillet, heat oil; separate onion slices into rings and dip them into the batter. Fry rings in hot oil until a light golden color.

Place on paper towel. Keep in warm oven.

Sprinkle with salt just before serving time. Serves 6.

CEVICHE

Marinated Fish

This entree is from Peru. Serve it with corn on the cob and sweet potato on a bed of leaf lettuce. You will find it very refreshing in the summer time.

2 lbs of fresh flounder (or mackerel) fillets
1-1/2 tsp salt
1/4 tsp freshly ground black pepper
1/4 cup fresh lemon juice
1 cup fresh lime juice
1 clove garlic, minced
1/2 cup onion, finely chopped
1/4 cup bell pepper, finely chopped
1/4 cup hot pepper, finely chopped
1/4 cup culantro, freshly chopped

Cut flounder fillets in very small cubes. Add salt, pepper, juice of lime, lemon, garlic. Place in refrigerator overnight, turning several times. Juices will cook fish. Two hours before serving time, add onion, bell pepper and hot pepper. Garnish with culantro. Serves 12.

PIZZA CAROLITA

Caroline's Pizza Pie

USA/Children's favorite at birthday parties, Perú

1 pkg dry gran yeast
1 cup lukewarm water
2 tsp sugar
1-1/2 tsp salt
1 tbsp veg oil
4 cups flour
Vegetable oil
2 6 oz- cans tomato sauce
1 lb mozarella cheese, sliced very thin
1/4 lb cooked hot pork sausage
1/2 cup chopped onion (sauted in oil)
2 tbsp Parmesan cheese
Salt, pepper
1 tbsp oregano

Turn dry granular yeast into 1/4 cup of the water and soften 10 minutes. Put remaining water into large bowl, add sugar, salt, oil and 1 cup of the flour and beat until smooth. Beat in yeast mixture.

Now stir in remaining flour to make a stiff dough. Turn out on floured board and knead until smooth, about 10 minutes. Return to

washed, greased bowl, turn once to bring greased side up. Cover and let rise in warm place until double, about 1 hr. Cut into 4 portions, cover. Let rest 10 minutes.

Place one portion of dough at a time on Pizza pans and press into 12-inch circles. Brush dough with oil. Spread tomato sauce on the four circles of dough.

Place mozarella cheese, then cooked sausage which has been sliced very thin, onion and grated Parmesan cheese. Season with salt, pepper and oregano.

Bake immediately in very hot oven (450°) until done, about 20 minutes.

Cut in wedges. Serves 8 to 10.

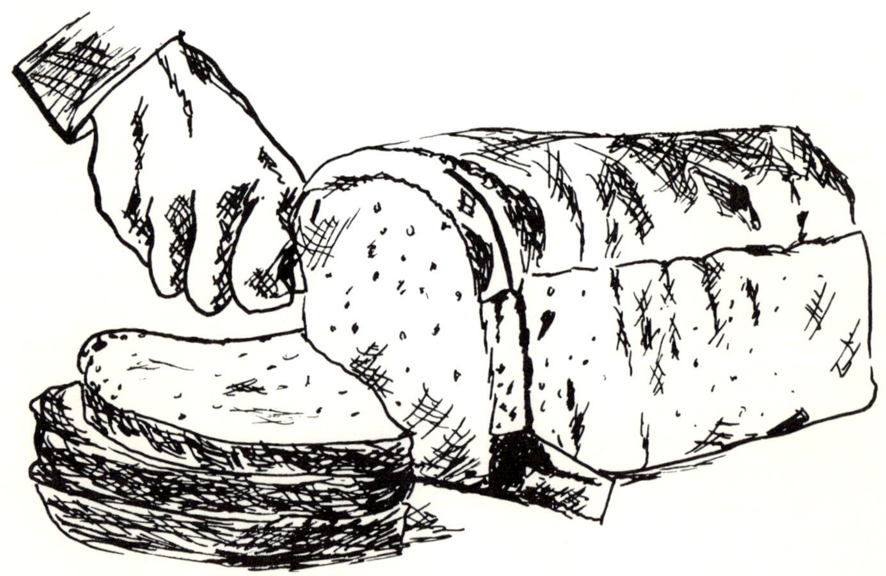

Breads

PANECITOS DE FIESTA

Fiesta Rolls

Freshly baked rolls from Latin America

8 cups unbleached sifted flour
2 pkgs dry granular yeast
1/4 cup lukewarm water
1 tsp sugar
2 cups low fat milk, scalded
2 tsp salt
1/4 cup sugar
2 eggs
1/3 cup veg oil

Place yeast into lukewarm water, stir in the teaspoon sugar; let it soften for about 15 minutes.

In large pan heat milk with salt and sugar and cool to lukewarm. Add yeast mixture, eggs and mix well. Beat in half the flour, then the oil. Stir in all but 1/4 cup of remaining flour and mix in thoroughly with wooden spoon.

Turn out on floured counter and cover dough with bowl. Let it rest 15 minutes. Now knead until dough is smooth, about 10 minutes.

Place in greased bowl, turning dough once, so that all sides of dough are greasy. Cover with clean dish towel, let it rise in warm place until double, about 2 hours.

Punch down and turn dough over, cover and again let it rise until double.

Press dough out onto floured counter, about 1/2 inch thick. Cut out with floured biscuit cutter into 48 rolls.

Sprinkle corn meal on large cookie sheet and place rolls next to each other, touching sides. Brush rolls lightly with vegetable oil. Place cookie sheet in warm place for about 2 hours.

Bake in 400° oven 12 minutes or until rolls are a nice golden color.

Makes 4 dozen rolls. Freezes well.

PAN DE MIEL Y AVENA

Johnny's Oatmeal–Honey Bread

5 cups unbleached flour
2-1/2 cups quick Quaker Oats
1/3 cup honey
2 tsp salt
3 tbsp veg oil
1-1/4 cups boiling water
1 pkg dry gran yeast
1 tsp. sugar
1/4 cup lukewarm water
1 tsp honey
1 cup nonfat milk, scalded

Sift flour. In large bowl place next four ingredients. Pour boiling water over this mixture and stir well with wooden spoon. Leave soaking till ready to use. Add yeast and 1 teaspoon of sugar to lukewarm water, stir and let it soften for 10 minutes.

To lukewarm milk, add yeast and add to oatmeal mixture. Mix in about 2 cups of flour, stirring well with wooden spoon. Add the remaining flour, saving about 1/3 cup.

Turn out on kitchen counter which has been sprinkled with remaining flour. Cover dough with bowl. Let it rest for 5 minutes, then knead until very elastic, about 12 minutes.

Place in greased bowl, turning once to bring greased side up. Cover, let rise in warm place until double, about 2 hours.

Cut in half, round up into 2 balls and cover again with bowl. Let rest 5 minutes. Shape into 2 loaves as follows:

1. Stretch dough with hands into a rectangular shape about 6x10-inches.
2. Fold long edge nearest to you over to center and seal carefully.
3. Fold long edge farthest from you over to center and seal carefully.
4. Lift folded dough up by both ends and stretch by slapping against counter top a couple of times, until it is double in size.
5. Bring ends of dough to the center and press together gently to seal.
6. Fold over the edge of dough nearest to you over to center and seal.
7. Fold over the edge of dough farthest from you over to center and seal.
8. Roll dough very carefully back and forth with palms of hands to round the loaves.
9. Place in greased loaf pans with seam side down.
10. Cover loaves with damp cloth and let it rise in warm place until double.

Bake in 350° oven for 40 minutes. Remove from pans immediately. Cool.

Makes 2 loaves.

PAN DE CAMOTE Y MIEL

Sweet Potato-Honey Bread

8 cups unbleached flour
2 pkgs dry gran yeast
1/4 cup lukewarm water
1/4 cup honey
2 cups nonfat milk, scalded
1 tsp salt
1-3/4 cups sweet potato, cooked
1/4 cup veg oil

Sift flour. Dissolve granular yeast into lukewarm water with 1 teaspoon honey and let it soften for 10 minutes.

Pour lukewarm milk, honey, salt and sweet potato in blender. Blend till creamy. Add yeast.

Pour this milk mixture into large bowl, adding 2 cups of flour, stirring well with wooden spoon until smooth. Now add veg oil and rest of flour, saving about 1/3 cup.

Turn out on kitchen counter which has been sprinkled with remaining flour. Cover dough with bowl. Let it rest for 5 minutes, then knead until very elastic, about 12 minutes.

Place in greased bowl, turning once to bring greased side up. Cover, let rise in warm place until double, about 2 hours.

Round up into 3 balls and cover again with bowl. Let rest 5 minutes. Shape into 3 loaves, page 24.

Bake in 350° oven for 40 minutes. Remove from pans immediately to cool.

Makes 3 loaves.

PAN MEJICANO

Mexican Corn Bread

2 tbsp veg oil
1 cup yellow corn meal
1 cup unbleached flour
3 tbsp sugar
4 tsp baking powder
1/2 tsp salt
1/4 tsp garlic powder
1/4 tsp Cayenne pepper
1 egg
1 cup skimmed milk
1/4 cup veg oil

Start oven 10 minutes before baking; set to 425°.

Pour two tablespoons oil inside an 8-inch square aluminum pan. Place in hot oven to heat thoroughly.

Sift first seven ingredients. Mix egg, milk and oil and add to dry ingredients. Mix with fork until ingredients are well blended.

Pour this mixture in hot aluminum pan. Bake for 20 minutes or till corn bread has a rich golden color.

Serves 6.

PANECITOS PARA EL TE

Tea Biscuits / Lima

These are often served at tea parties.

2 cups all purpose flour
3 tsp baking powder
1 tsp salt
1/3 cup veg oil
2/3 cup nonfat milk (liquid)

Heat oven to 475°. Sift dry ingredients into bowl.

Measure oil and milk in measuring cup, without stirring. Pour into flour and stir with wooden spoon until mixture cleans sides of bowl.

Place in 8"x8"x2" aluminum pan. Pat out 1-inch thick.

Bake 12 to 15 minutes or until golden brown. Cut into 3x2-inch rectangles.

Serve hot. Serves 6.

PANECILLOS ABUELITA

Grandma's Muffins

We made these muffins in Panama on Christmas Eve and try to continue the tradition each year.

1-1/4 cups nonfat milk
3/4 tsp salt
1 pkg dry gran yeast
1/4 cup lukewarm water
1 tsp sugar
4 cups unbleached flour
3 tbsp veg oil
Corn meal

Scald milk with salt and cool to lukewarm in large bowl.

Mix granular yeast into the lukewarm water, stir in sugar and let it soften 10 min. Stir yeast mixture into milk, adding half the flour gradually, mixing well with wooden spoon until batter is well mixed. Add vegetable oil and rest of flour and continue mixing with spoon until dough is smooth.

Turn dough into greased bowl. Cover and let rise in warm place until double, about 2 hrs. Turn out on floured counter and knead well. Cover with bowl and let it rest 10 min. Now roll out 1/2-inch thick.

Cut into 4-inch rounds and place on cookie sheet, which has been sprinkled with corn meal. Let it rise in warm place until muffins start getting light, about 50 min.

Heat large frying pan which has been lightly greased with oil. Saute 4 or 5 muffins at a time for about 20 minutes turning 2 or 3 times.

Split muffins and spread with butter. About 14 muffins.

PANECITOS DE LAS 5

5 o'clock rolls

8-1/2 cups unbleached flour
2 pks dry gran yeast
1 cup lukewarm water
1/4 cup sugar
2 cups scalded nonfat milk
4-1/2 tsp salt
4 tbsp veg oil

Combine yeast, lukewarm water, sugar, and let it stand 5 minutes to soften.

Scald milk with salt and place in a very large bowl. Cool to lukewarm. Add yeast mixture and 3 cups of the flour. Mix with wooden spoon until smooth. Add oil and mix well. Add remaining flour and continue to mix until smooth.

Turn out on floured counter and knead dough for about 10 minutes. Place dough in a large greased bowl, turning dough over, making sure dough is well greased (or oiled) on all sides.

Cover bowl with dish towel and let it rise for 2 hours. Now punch dough and turn over. Cover and let it rise 1 more hour.

Place dough on floured counter and roll to about 1 inch thick. Cut dough into 24 small circles. Place on greased baking sheet which has been sprinkled with corn meal.

Bake in a 400° oven for 20 minutes or until a light golden color.

Makes 2 dozen rolls. Freezes well.

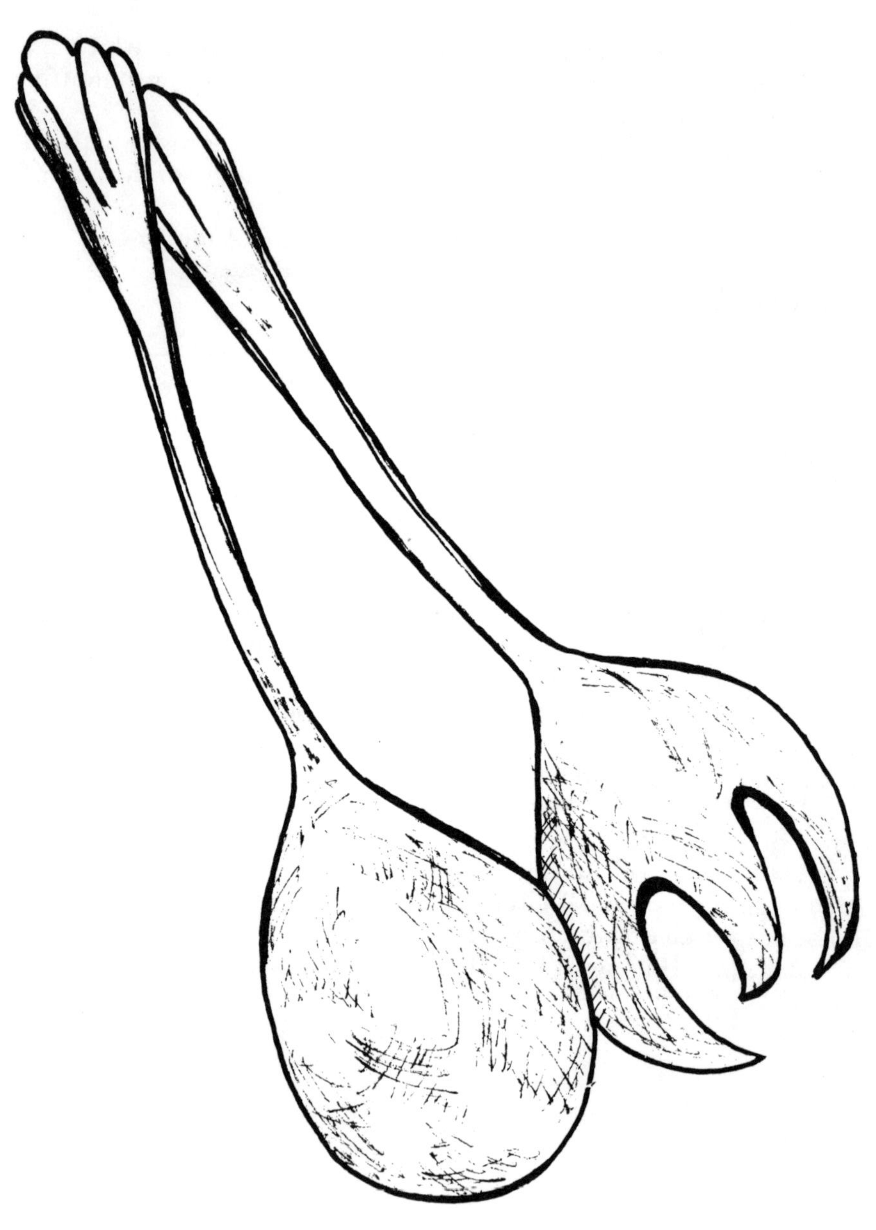

Salads and Dressings

ENSALADA DE PALTA

Avocado Salad, Dominica

2 medium size ripe avocados
1 medium size onion, chopped fine
2 ripe tomatoes, diced
Salt, pepper
1/4 cup Vilma's Salad Dressing #1
Lettuce Leaves

Peel and dice avocado. Add next 4 ingredients and mix with wooden spoon carefully.

Place 1/2 cup of this mixture on lettuce leaves. Serves 5.

SALSA DE TOMATE PARA ENSALADA

Tomato Dressing

1-1/2 cups veg oil
1/2 cup cider vinegar
1/3 cup water
2 tsp salt
3 tbsp catsup
1 tsp onion powder
1/2 tsp garlic powder
1 tbsp honey

Put all ingredients in blender and blend for 1 minute. Pour this dressing into a large jar. Keep covered in refrigerator.

Use as needed.

SALSA CRUDA PICANTE

Hot Uncooked Tomato Sauce

This sauce is very tasty on meat. Honduras.

2 ripe tomatoes
1 tsp hot pepper, chopped
1 medium size onion, chopped
4 radishes, chopped fine
1 tsp culantro (Chinese parsley)
1 tsp olive oil
Salt, pepper, to taste

Peel tomatoes and chop fine.

Mix with rest of ingredients and place in a small deep bowl to accompany meats.

Makes 1-1/2 cups.

CHIRMOL

Doña Lita's Radishes

Doña Lita, from Honduras, made my mouth water every time she spoke of "Chirmol" radishes. These should be served with pork, beans, and cassava.

1 small package radishes, about 25
1 medium size onion, chopped
1 tomato, peeled, chopped
Juice of 1 lemon
1 tsp apple cider vinegar
1/4 tsp cumin powder
1 tsp fresh culantro, chopped
1/2 tsp veg oil
1 tsp hot sauce
Salt, pepper

Wash radishes well.

Slice very thin and mix with rest of ingredients. Makes 1-1/2 cups.

ENSALADA DE POLLO COPACABANA

Chicken Salad

Copacabana, Brazil

2 cups cold cooked chicken meat, cubed
1/2 cup mayonnaise
1/2 cup diced celery
1 small onion, chopped
1/2 cup walnuts, chopped
Salt, pepper
Lettuce
Hearts of palm

Mix chicken with next 5 ingredients.

Serve on lettuce leaves. Garnish with hearts of palm. Serves 6.

ENSALADA DE CARNAVAL

Carnival Bean Salad

Brazil

2 cups green beans, cut into 2-inch pieces
1/4 cup water
1 15 oz can red kidney beans, drained
1 medium size onion, chopped
5 radishes, washed and chopped very fine
1/2 cup Vilma's salad dressing #2
Lettuce leaves

Place green beans in covered saucepan with 1/4 cup water. Let it come to a boil. Lower heat and cook for 5 minutes. Leave beans in covered pan to cook in their own steam for another 10 minutes. There shouldn't be any water left over.

Place drained green beans, kidney beans, onion and radishes in salad bowl. Add salad dressing and mix thoroughly. Place salad in refrigerator for several hours before serving time.

Serve on a bed of lettuce leaves. Serves 6.

SALSA VILMA #1

Vilma's Salad Dressing #1

This tasty salad dressing can be kept in the refrigerator and contains no preservatives.

1-1/2 cups vegetable oil
1/2 cup apple cider vinegar
1/3 cups water
1 tsp honey
2 tsp salt
1/4 tsp each, Cayenne pepper, garlic powder
1 tbsp onion powder
2 tbsp grated Parmesan cheese
1/4 cup nonfat milk powder (optional)

Place all ingredients in blender. Blend at high speed for 1 minute.

Place in large jar.

Keep covered in refrigerator. Use as needed.

SALSA VILMA #2

Vilma's Salad Dressing #2

This salad dressing is sweetened with a ripe apple.

1-1/2 cups veg oil
1/2 cup apple cider vinegar
1/3 cup water
1 small ripe apple, cut in quarters, cored
2 tsp salt
1/2 tsp each, Cayenne pepper, garlic powder
1 tbsp onion powder
1 tbsp fresh parsley
1 tbsp grated Parmesan cheese

Place all ingredients in blender. Blend at high speed for 1 minute or until well blended.

Place in large jar. Keep covered in refrigerator.

Use as needed.

ENSALADA MIXTA

Mixed Green Salad

2 cups spinach leaves
4 large Boston lettuce leaves
2 Romaine lettuce leaves
6 radishes
1 ripe avocado, peeled, diced

Wash first four ingredients.

Drain well. Tear spinach and lettuce leaves in bite-size pieces. Slice radishes very thin. Place in bowl in refrigerator.

When ready to serve add diced avocado. Pour 1/3 cup Vilma's Salad Dressing #1 on all ingredients.

Toss well and serve immediately.

Serves 6 to 8

ENSALADA DE PESCADO CON NUECES
Tuna Fish Salad with Walnuts

2 6-1/2 oz. cups tuna fish
1/3 cup mayonnaise
1/2 cup grated carrot
1 small onion, chopped
1/2 cup walnuts, chopped
Salt, pepper
Lettuce
Olives

Drain cans of tuna fish and mix with next 5 ingredients.

Serve on a bed of lettuce leaves.

Garnish with olives. Serves 6.

ENSALADA DE PAPAS JUANITA
Potato Salad Juanita

My mother will always be remembered for her delicious potato salad. Peru.

6 med. size potatoes
2 med. size carrots
1/2 cup sweet peas (optional)
1/3 cup olive oil
1 onion, chopped fine
1/3 cup imitation mayonnaise
1/4 cup lime juice
Salt, pepper, to taste
2 anchovies, chopped
1 hard boiled egg

Cook potatoes, carrots and peas until tender. Drain. Refrigerate.

In medium size pan heat oil; in it saute onion until soft.

Place onion in large bowl with mayonnaise, lime juice, salt, pepper and mix well. Add peeled cubed potatoes and carrots. Add peas and anchovies. Mix all ingredients with wooden spoon.

Garnish with sliced egg.

Serves 6.

PAPAS A LA HUANCAINA

Potatoes with Cheese Sauce

Very colorful, Peru.

6 med potatoes
16 oz low-fat cottage cheese
1/2 tsp Cayenne pepper
1 tsp salt
1/4 tsp pepper
1/2 tsp turmeric
3 tbsp evaporated skimmed milk
1/3 cup veg oil skimmed
2 tbsp onion, chopped
Lettuce leaves
3 hard boiled eggs
Olives

Cook potatoes in salted water until tender.

Peel and refrigerate.

In blender, mix cottage cheese, seasonings, milk, oil and onion. Blend till very creamy.

Arrange lettuce leaves on platter, place potatoes cut in half over them. Pour cheese sauce on top.

Garnish with slivered eggs, and olives.

Serves 8 to 10.

ENSALADA DE PEPINO

Cucumber Salad

At a very cozy restaurant in Miraflores, our family enjoyed this salad. Peru.

3 medium size cucumbers
1/3 cup mayonnaise
1 tbsp lemon juice
1 tsp salt

Wash and slice cucumbers very thin.

Mix next 3 ingredients and pour over cucumber slices.

Mix well and refrigerate until serving time.

Serves 4.

CAUSA A LA LIMEÑA

Lima Potatoes with Onion Sauce

Peru.

1 onion, chopped fine
Juice of 2 lemons
2 tsp salt
Pepper
1 tsp hot pepper, seeded, chopped
8 medium size potatoes, peeled, cubed
1/2 cup olive oil

Marinate the onion with lemon juice, salt, pepper, hot pepper, for 1 hour. Set aside.

In the meantime, boil potatoes in small amount of water, in covered pan, (water should have evaporated at the end of cooking time, about 20 minutes). Mash potatoes well. Add marinated onions and oil. Mix well with wooden spoon.

Shape potato mixture in small flat cakes.

ONION SAUCE FOR LIMA POTATOES

1 onion, sliced fine
1/2 tsp fresh hot pepper, seeded, chopped
1/4 cup Vilma's Salad Dressing #1

Wash onion slices. Drain.

Mix onion with rest of ingredients and pour over potato patties.

Serve on a bed of lettuce, with corn on the cob, diced farmer's cheese, and olives.

Serves 6.

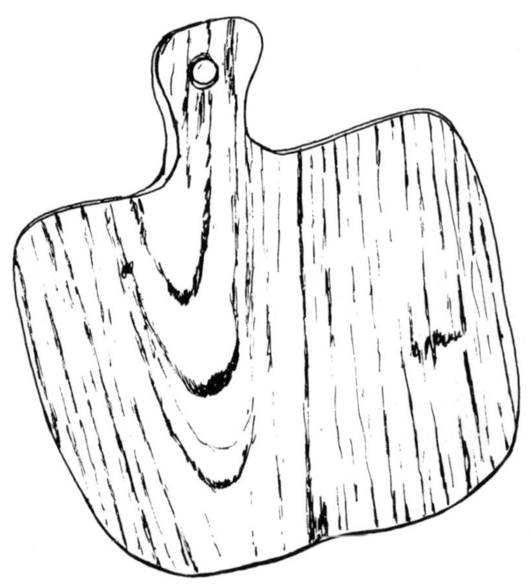

Soups

SOPA DE BOLITAS DE CARNE Y ESPINACA

Spinach–Meat Ball Soup

Chile.

1/2 lb lean ground meat
2 tbsp veg oil
1 clove garlic, minced
4 scallions, chopped
1 tsp toasted sesame seeds
4 tbsp Soy sauce
Salt, pepper
6 cups water
1 tbsp cornstarch dissolved in
 1/4 cup cold water
3 cups fresh, washed spinach
 (1/2 lb.)

Shape ground meat into tiny meat balls and fry in hot frying pan until brown on all sides. Throw away the fat.

To same frying pan, add vegetable oil, garlic, scallions, sesame seeds and saute for 10 minutes. Add Soy sauce, salt, pepper, water and cornstarch paste. Cook soup allowing it to boil slowly over medium heat (about 15 minutes.)

Add spinach and continue cooking for 2 more minutes.

Serves 6.

SOPA DE POLLO Y APIO

Chicken–Celery Soup

Guatemala.

6 cups water
2 breasts of chicken
2 chicken backs, necks, gizzards
1 onion
Salt, pepper
1 clove garlic, minced
1/2 tsp ginger powder
2 cabbage leaves
1 cup finely chopped celery
3 tbsp corn starch
1/2 cup cold water
Soy sauce
Chopped scallions

In large saucepan, put water and next seven ingredients. Cook for one hour. Strain and save chicken stock.

Debone chicken breasts. Chop breast meat fine. Set aside.

Add finely chopped celery to chicken stock plus corn starch which has been diluted in cold water. Let it all come to a full boil. Simmer, stirring with wooden spoon till soup is clear.

Add chopped breast of chicken to soup. Season with Soy sauce. Garnish with chopped scallions.
Serves 6.

SOPA DE ARVEJAS SECAS

Split Pea Soup

Argentina

1 8 oz bag split peas
5 cups water
1 ham bone
1 onion, chopped
1 carrot, sliced
1 tbsp salt
1/4 tsp ground pepper
1/4 tsp ground ginger
1/4 tsp thyme
1/4 tsp garlic powder
3 tbsp margarine
1-1/4 cups dry bread cubes

Wash split peas. Place them with water, ham bone, onion, carrot and seasonings in large pot. Bring water to a boil.

Cover and simmer 1-1/4 hours, stirring occasionally so that ingredients do not stick to pan.

Just before serving time, melt margarine in frying pan. Stir in bread cubes and continue stirring over low heat until lightly toasted.

Keep warm in oven.

When soup is ready to be served, ladle into soup bowls and garnish with croutons. Serves 6 to 8.

SOPA DE CHILCANO

Fish Soup

This is a rich fish soup from Peru.

2 lbs fresh whole mackerel
5 cups water
2 tbsp veg oil
1 onion, chopped
1/4 tsp fresh hot pepper, cut in thin strips
Salt, pepper to taste
1/2 tsp oregano
1 tbsp parsley, chopped
3 large potatoes, cubed
Lime juice, to taste

Clean fish and cook in 5 cups water for 20 minutes. Strain and save stock. In large skillet, heat oil; in it saute onion until tender. Add seasonings, potatoes, fish stock and cook 20 minutes longer.

Season with salt, pepper and lime juice.

Place small chunks of cooked mackerel in soup bowls. Serves 6.

SOPA DE FRIJOLES
Bean Soup

In Bolivia they warm up with a bowl of bean soup.

1 cup leftover chili con carne, with beans
4 cups water
1 cup cooked broad noodles

Place chili and water in blender. Blend for one minute.

Pour into pan and heat thoroughly. Add cooked warm noodles to soup.

Serves 5.

GAZPACHO DE LIS
Lis's Cold Tomato Soup

Many of Lis's Latin American friends gathered at her house to sample this colorful soup.

3 slices white bread
1 tbsp salt
1 tsp cumin powder
2 tbsp veg oil
1/4 tsp garlic powder
6 med size tomatoes, quartered
3 cups cold water
1/8 tsp pepper
1/8 tsp Cayenne pepper
2 tbsp apple cider vinegar

Garnish
2 slices white bread, toasted, buttered and cut up in very small cubes
2 peeled tomatoes, diced fine
1 cucumber, chopped very fine
1 small onion, chopped fine

Put first six ingredients in blender. Blend till creamy. Add cold water, pepper, Cayenne pepper and vinegar. Mix well.

Place in large bowl in refrigerator and chill.

When ready to serve, place garnish in "Lazy Susan" with individual teaspoons in center of table.

Pour chilled soup into soup bowl. Each person can garnish their own soup bowl. Serves 6.

SOPA DE TOMATE RIO BLANCO CON CUBITOS DE PAN TOSTADO

Rio Blanco Tomato Soup

In the cool, crisp air of Rio Blanco's mining town, we savored this soup. Peru.

3-1/2 cups canned peeled tomatoes
1 tbsp parsley, chopped
1/2 bay leaf
1/4 tsp basil
1/4 tsp fresh ground pepper
1 tbsp onion, chopped
1-1/2 tsp sugar
1 tsp salt
2 cups water mixed with
2 tbsp corn starch
3 whole cloves
2 tbsp margarine

Put all ingredients in blender, except for whole cloves and margarine. Pour into saucepan with cloves. Bring to a boil, stirring constantly. Simmer 15 minutes longer.

Strain.

Add margarine and stir till it melts. Serve with croutons if desired.

Serve hot. Serves 6.

CUBITOS DE PAN TOSTADOS

Croutons

4 slices bread
2 tbsp margarine
2 tbsp veg oil

Spread bread slices with margarine. Cut in small cubes. In medium size frying pan saute bread cubes until a golden brown.

Use as garnish for soups.

CHUPE DE PESCADO

Fish Chowder

A nutritious fish soup from Peru.

1 very large fish head
1 branch celery
6 cups water
2 tbsp veg oil
1 onion, chopped
3 cloves garlic, minced
1 cup tomato sauce
1 tbsp parsley, chopped
Salt, pepper, to taste
1/4 tsp cayenne pepper
1/2 tsp oregano
2 potatoes, cubed
1/4 cup raw white rice
1/2 lb flounder fillets
Flour, veg oil
1/2 cup clean raw shrimp
1/2 cup evaporated milk
3 hard boiled eggs
Parsley, chopped (1 tbsp)

In large pan place clean fish head, celery and water. Boil covered for 20 minutes. Strain well and set aside.

In large pan, heat oil; in it saute onion, garlic, till tender, about 10 minutes. Add next five ingredients. Simmer 5 minutes.

Add fish stock, potatoes, rice and let it simmer, covered, for 20 minutes

Cut flounder fillets in squares. Roll in flour. Fry in oil to a golden color. Set these aside.

Add shrimp to soup, cover and simmer for 10 more minutes. Turn heat off. Add evaporated milk.

Place half a boiled egg and fried fish in each soup bowl.

Garnish with chopped parsley. Serves 6. Freezes well.

SOPA TEOLOGA

A one meal Chicken Soup

Peru.

1 3 lb chicken
1-1/2 qts water
2 onions
1/2 tsp oregano
1 tsp salt
1/4 tsp pepper
1 tbsp veg oil
1 tbsp parsley, chopped
2 cloves garlic, chopped
1/2 tsp dry basil
1 carrot, sliced fine
3 med potatoes, cubed
2 tbsp tomato sauce
8 pitted olives
2 hard boiled eggs
7 slices bread, toasted, cubed

In large saucepan, place clean chicken, water, one onion, oregano, salt and pepper. Bring to a boil. Simmer covered for 1-1/2 hours. Skim off fat, if desired.

Lift chicken into platter and save stock. Debone and skin chicken. Set aside.

In small skillet, heat oil; in it saute 1 chopped onion, parsley, garlic, basil. Add carrot, potatoes, and tomato sauce. Cook covered, 15 minutes or until tender.

Place an olive, egg sliver, cubed toasted bread, chicken pieces into soup bowls before serving. Serves 6 to 8.

SOPA GAUCHA DE ZAPALLO

Pumpkin Soup

In Argentina they serve this hearty soup with diced fresh cheese.

1 lb fresh pumpkin, peeled and cubed
4 cups water
2 tbsp veg oil
1 small onion, chopped
1 clove garlic, minced
1 tbsp tomato sauce
1 cup evaporated skimmed milk
1-1/2 tsp salt
Pepper
1 tbsp parsley, chopped
1/2 cup Farmer's style cheese, diced

Place pumpkin in water and cook until tender.

In small saucepan, heat oil; in it saute onion, and garlic, till tender.

Add tomato sauce, milk, salt, pepper and add to cooked pumpkin. Pour this mixture in blender and blend for 1 minute.

Serve this soup in small individual soup bowls. Garnish with parsley and diced cheese.

Serves 4.

Seafood

ENSOPADO DE PESCADO CON CAMARON

Flounder with Shrimp Sauce

El Salvador

1 lb flounder fillets
1/4 cup veg oil
1 onion, chopped
2 tbsp bell pepper, chopped
1 lb canned tomatoes
1 clove garlic, minced
1 bay leaf
1/4 tsp each, Cayenne pepper, thyme
1 cup thinly sliced carrots
1 tsp flour
1 tsp corn starch
1/2 cup cold water
1 cup fresh clean shrimps
2 tbsp evaporated skimmed milk

Lay fillets on greased baking pan. Brush well with 1 tablespoon oil. Place under broiler, about 2 inches below flame, cook until fish is done but still moist (about 10 minutes). Set aside.

In heavy skillet, heat oil, in it saute onion until tender. Add bell pepper, tomatoes, seasonings, carrots and simmer 20 minutes. Add flour and corn starch which have been diluted in the water, stirring constantly till thickened. Add shrimp and simmer 10 minutes longer. Add evaporated milk and stir well.

Pour this shrimp mixture over fish fillets.

Serve with rice or mashed potatoes. Serves 6.

CALAMARES FRITOS CON VERDURAS

Squids—Fried with Vegetables

I cannot ever fix enough squid for my family. They love it! Peru.

2 lbs squid
4 tsp veg oil
2 onions, sliced lengthwise
2 cloves garlic, minced
1 bell pepper, cut in thin strips
1 bunch scallions, sliced in two inch strips
1 tsp paprika
Salt, pepper
Soy sauce, Cayenne pepper

Clean squid and debone. Cut it up in thin strips. In heavy iron skillet heat oil; in it saute squid, onions and garlic for about 10 minutes.

Add bell pepper, scallions, paprika, salt and pepper and stir fry for 3 minutes.

Season with Soy sauce and Cayenne pepper, to taste.

Serves 6.

TRUCHA DE MAR ASADA A LA CRIOLLA

Creole Baked Sea Trout

Grenada.

1 5 lb sea trout (whole)
4 tbsp lemon juice
4 tsp salt
1 tsp garlic powder
1 tsp oregano
1/4 tsp Cayenne pepper
4 tbsp olive oil
2 medium size onions, chopped
1/2 cup tomato sauce
1/2 cup white wine
1 tbsp parsley, chopped

Clean and wash fish in cold water. Dry with paper towel. Rub lemon juice, salt, garlic powder, oregano and Cayenne pepper all over fish, inside and out.

Place fish in refrigerator for 1/2 an hour so that seasonings will improve fish flavor. Line a large pan with aluminum foil.

Mix rest of ingredients, and pour only half of these ingredients on bottom of aluminum lined pan.

Now, place whole fish over this mixture and cover fish with remaining onion mix.

Bake uncovered in a 375° oven for about 40 minutes. Do not overcook. Fish should be moist and flaky.

Place fish carefully on large platter, with two spatulas. Garnish with lots of parsley.

Serves 6.

CROQUETAS DE MAR

Clam Tuna Cakes

These cakes can be shaped a bit smaller, and served as an appetizer. Brazil.

1 8 oz can minced clams
1 7 oz can solid light tuna
1 egg
2 cups fine saltine cracker crumbs
1/4 cup clam juice
1/4 tsp pepper
1/4 tsp garlic powder
1/4 tsp Cayenne pepper

Mix all ingredients thoroughly. Form into egg shaped balls. Fry in deep veg oil until golden brown.
Serves 4.

FILETE DE LENGUADO Y CAMARON BAIANO

Fillet of Flounder and Shrimp

From Bahia.

4 tbsp veg oil
1/4 cup chopped onion
3 tbsp flour
1-1/2 tsp salt
1-1/2 cups milk
1/4 tsp Cayenne pepper
1/4 tsp garlic powder
2 tsp parsley, chopped
1/2 tsp capers
1 lb fillet of flounder (sole or turbot)
1 cup cooked shrimps
1/2 cup bread crumbs
1/4 cup Parmesan cheese

In heavy skillet, heat oil; in it saute onion till tender. Add flour and stir well. Add salt, milk, Cayenne pepper, garlic, parsley, capers. Simmer, stirring constantly until thickened.

Place fillet of flounder in this sauce, cover and simmer 10 minutes.

Place fish in glass baking dish, cover with sauce, shrimps, bread crumbs, Parmesan cheese. Broil till crumbs are crispy and golden.

Serves 6.

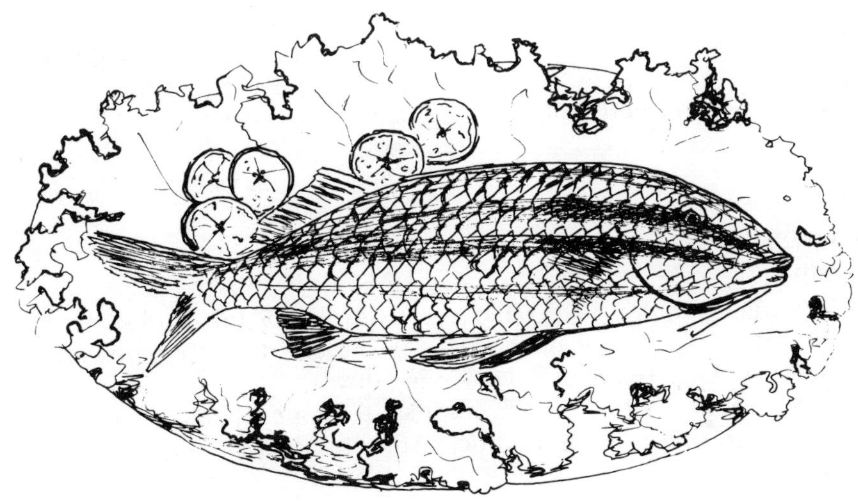

BACALAO ESTILO MAMAMA

Dry Cod "Mamama's" Style

"Bacalao" has always been eaten at our house on Good Friday as a tradition in our family. Peru.

1/2 lb dry salted codfish
1/3 cup olive oil
2 onions, chopped
2 cloves garlic, minced
1 8 oz can tomato sauce
1 small jar red bell peppers
8 pitted olives
1 bay leaf
1/4 tsp Cayenne pepper
1/4 cup burgundy wine
4 large potatoes, cooked, peeled and sliced

Soak codfish in cold water overnight, changing water three times. Drain and flake fish very fine. In large skillet, heat oil; in it fry codfish until lightly browned. Add onions, garlic and saute 10 minutes. Add tomato sauce, bell peppers, olives, bay leaf, cayenne pepper and wine.

In large rectangular Pyrex dish, place layers of cooked sliced potatoes and codfish mixture, ending with codfish mixture.

Place in 325° oven and bake 1 hour.

Serves 6.

ESCABECHE DE LENGUADO

Marinated Flounder

Honduras.

1/4 cup veg oil
Flour
6 med size fish fillets (sole, sea trout, etc.)
Salt, pepper
2 tbsp veg oil
2 onions, sliced
1 bell pepper, cut in thin rings
1 clove garlic, finely chopped
1 hot pepper, sliced fine
1/4 tsp. oregano
Salt, pepper
1/4 cup wine vinegar
Lettuce leaves
Green pitted olives
Hard boiled eggs

In large skillet, heat oil. Flour fish fillets lightly and saute them until delicately brown on both sides. Season to taste with salt and pepper. Arrange fillets in a flat serving dish.

In a heavy skillet heat oil; in it saute onions, pepper rings, garlic, hot pepper, oregano, until tender. Add salt, pepper, vinegar and let it all come to a boil.

Immediately pour this onion mixture on top of fish fillets.

Garnish platter with rest of ingredients. Serves 6. Serve cold with corn on the cob.

PASTEL DE SALMON

Salmon Shell Pie

It is great as a main luncheon dish. Chile.

2 cups unbleached flour
1 tsp salt
7 tbsp shortening
1/3 cup ice water
4 tbsp veg oil
1 medium onion, chopped
3 cloves garlic, minced
1 tbsp parsley, chopped
4 tbsp flour
1 lb can pink salmon
1-1/2 cups nonfat milk
Salt, pepper
1-1/2 tbsp lemon juice

Sift flour with salt. Cut in shortening with 2 knives until mixture resembles rice grains. Add water all at once, stirring quickly with a fork until dough just stiffens.

Divide dough in half. Roll each half out into a circle on wax paper and give it the shape of a sea shell or fish. Place one side of pie shell which has been formed on wax paper in refrigerator. Place second shell on aluminum sheet and spread cool filling over it. About 1/2-inch from edge. Wet edge with cold water. Now turn second shell-shape from waxed paper over filling. Press edges together to seal.

Mark flutings around sea shell and with a knive make lengthwise markings to resemble a sea shell..

Bake 15 minutes in 450° oven then reduce heat to 350° and bake 30 minutes longer.

Slide out onto platter.

Garnish with parsley and serve hot. Serves 8.

Filling

In medium size pan heat oil; in it saute onion, garlic and parsley until tender. Add flour and mix well. Add salmon with its juice, milk, salt, pepper and stir well.

Cook over medium heat, stirring constantly until it thickens.

Cover and simmer 10 more minutes.

Add lemon juice.

Let it cool before filling shell.

PESCADO FRITO

Fried Crispy Fish

Fresh fish is plentiful in Barbados.

6 fish fillets
1 tbsp lemon juice
1 tsp onion powder
Salt, pepper
1/2 cup unbleached flour
2 tsp baking powder
1/2 cup water
1/2 cup veg oil

Season fish fillets with lemon juice, onion powder, salt, pepper.

In large soup bowl, mix flour, baking powder, water and pour over fish.

In large skillet, heat oil, pan-fry each fish fillet to a light golden color, on both sides.

Place on paper towel to drain a few seconds. Serve hot.

Serves 6.

BACALAO DE BAHIA

Cod from Bahia

4 med potatoes
2 lbs fresh cod fillets
1 tsp salt
1/4 tsp pepper
1/3 cup veg oil
1/2 cup onion, chopped
4 oz tomato sauce
1 tbsp bell pepper, chopped
1/4 tsp garlic powder
1/2 tsp capers
1/4 tsp sugar
2 tbsp parsley, chopped
1 bay leaf
1/4 tsp each, oregano, thyme, basil
6 pitted green olives
1/2 cup red cooking wine
Cooked peas, optional

Cook potatoes in boiling salted water till tender. Drain and peel potatoes. Cut in half then crosswise into thin slices.

Mix fish fillets with salt, pepper and 3 tablespoons of the oil.

Place in 2 baking dishes. Fry onions in remaining oil, till tender. Add tomato sauce, bell pepper, garlic, capers, sugar and seasonings. Cook for 5 minutes.

Add cooked sliced potatoes and simmer for 5 minutes longer. Add olives.

Arrange this mixture on top of fish fillets. Pour wine on top. Bake 20 minutes in 350° oven.

Garnish with peas if desired.

Serves 6 to 8.

Meat Cookery

TALLARINES GENOVESES

Spaghetti from Genova

1 lb spaghetti noodles
1/2 tsp salt
1/2 tsp veg oil
4 qts water
Parmesan cheese
Knockwurst (cooked)

Cook spaghetti in 4 qts boiling water, in which 1/2 teaspoon oil has been added. Cook until tender, about 12 minutes. Drain.

Pour green sauce over noodles. Garnish with Parmesan cheese and Knockwurst. Serves 6.

Salsa Verde Al Pesto

Green Sauce

If you cultivate your own basil in a garden, this sauce will taste even better!

1/2 tsp garlic powder
2 tbsp dried basil
1/4 cup Parmesan cheese
1/2 tsp salt
5 tbsp olive oil
1 cup finely chopped lettuce or French cut string beans
Parmesan cheese

Mix garlic, basil, cheese, salt. Gradually add oil, mixing well. On each plate, arrange mound of hot noodles, top with slightly cooked lettuce or well cooked string beans. Add 1 tablespoon green sauce.

Garnish with Parmesan cheese.

TALLARINES CON SALSA DE CARNE

Spaghetti with meat-tomato sauce

Many Monday evenings our family looked forward to "Spaghetti Night" at the Officer's Club in Panama. Jeanne's favorite!

1 lb spaghetti noodles
1/2 tsp salt
4 qts water
1/2 tsp veg oil
Parmesan cheese
meat tomato sauce

Cook noodles in 4 qts boiling water, in which 1/2 teaspoon oil has been added. Cook until tender, about 15 minutes.

Drain well.

Serve with meat tomato sauce. Sprinkle Parmesan cheese on top.

Serves 6.

Salsa de Carne Con Tomate

Meat—Tomato Sauce

1 tbsp veg oil
1 onion, chopped
1/4 tsp garlic powder
1 tbsp bell pepper, chopped
1 lb ground lean beef
1-1/2 tsp salt
1/4 tsp pepper
1 8 oz can tomato sauce
1 6 oz can tomato paste
1/4 tsp each, curry powder, oregano, basil, Cayenne pepper
1/2 bay leaf
1 carrot, finely chopped
1/2 tsp dried parsley
1/2 cup red Burgundy wine
1/2 cup orange juice

In large skillet, heat oil; in it saute onion, garlic, bell pepper until tender. Add ground beef and fry until lightly browned. Add salt, pepper, tomato sauce, tomato paste, seasonings, carrot, parsley and wine. Let it all come to a boil. Simmer for 30 minutes.

Add orange juice and simmer 15 minutes longer.

This sauce freezes well.

EMPANADAS

Meat Turnovers

These are traditionally served in Lima at receptions

2 cups unbleached flour
1 tsp salt
7 tbsp shortening
1/2 cup ice water
1 cup leftover thick meat spaghetti sauce
1/4 cup plump raisins
Olive slices
1 egg white
Veg oil

Sift flour with salt. Cut in shortening with 2 knives until mixture resembles rice grains. Add water all at once, stirring quickly with a fork until dough just stiffens. Place in covered container in refrigerator.

On lightly floured surface, roll out half the dough about 1/8" thick. Cut into rounds with a 3" cookie cutter. On half of each round place one teaspoon of meat sauce, 2 raisins and an olive slice. Brush edge of each round with egg white then fold over. Press edges together with tines of fork. Place on greased cookie sheet. Repeat with remaining dough.

Brush tops of Empanadas with vegetable oil. Bake in 450° oven for 20 minutes or till a golden color.

Serve warm. Makes about 2-1/2 dozen.

POLLO CON SALSA DE HONGOS

Chicken with Mushrooms

Paraguay

1 large chicken
2 cups water
3 tbsp veg oil
1 onion, chopped
2 cloves garlic, minced
2 medium size bell peppers, chopped
1 cup fresh mushrooms, sliced
1 tsp parsley, chopped
3 tbsp flour, dissolved in
3 tbsp water
2 cups chicken broth
1 cup skimmed evaporated milk
Salt, pepper

Boil chicken with two cups water in pressure cooker for 20 minutes. Let pressure go down normally. Place chicken on platter. Save broth. When cold, debone and discard skin. Cut chicken in bite size pieces.

In large size frying pan, place oil, onion, garlic and saute for 10 minutes. Add bell pepper, mushrooms, parsley, and saute 10 more minutes. Add flour paste and stir until well blended. Add chicken broth, milk, salt, pepper and mix well.

Simmer and stir with wooden spoon for 15 more minutes.

Serve with rice or noodles. Serves 6.

CANELONES

Cannelloni

You can substitute store bought noodles. Argentina.

1 recipe noodle dough, pg. 51
Corn starch
Boiling, salted water
2 cups Ricotta cheese (or cottage cheese)
3/4 cup grated Parmesan cheese
3/4 cup grated Mozarella cheese
1/3 cup evaporated skimmed milk
1/2 cup bread crumbs
1 large egg, beaten
Salt, pepper, to taste
2 cups well seasoned meat-tomato sauce
Grated Parmesan cheese
2-1/2 cups meat-tomato sauce (pg. 48)

Roll dough into a large thin rectangular sheet. Sprinkle with corn starch and fold in half. Roll again. Cut into 4x5-inch noodles.

Drop a few pieces at a time in boiling salted water for about 8 minutes. Rinse in cold water and drain well.. Combine Ricotta cheese with next five ingredients. Season with salt, pepper.

Pour 1/2 cup tomato sauce on bottom of large rectangular baking dish (about 14X10X2.)

Fill noodles with cheese mixture and place them, seam down, in baking pan. Top with tomato sauce. Sprinkle with grated Parmesan cheese.

Bake in 375° oven for 20 minutes.

Serves 6 to 8 and freezes well.

ÑOQUIS
Gnocchi

This is another of our favorites with meat-tomato sauce. Argentina.

4 medium potatoes, peeled
4 cups flour
2 tsp baking powder
Boiling water, with 1 tsp salt
Meat-tomato sauce, pg. 48
Parmesan cheese

Boil and mash potatoes. Sift baking powder with flour. Add to mashed potatoes. Knead until very smooth.

Roll dough into ropelike strips about 3/4-inch thick; cut into 3/4-inch pieces. Dip in flour. Use prong of fork to make dented design on each piece. Drop into boiling salted water and boil for about 8 minutes or until they rise to the surface. Drain quickly and place in a buttered pan.

Cover with meat tomato sauce and sprinkle Parmesan cheese on top.

Place in 350° oven and bake for half an hour.

Serves 6.

LASAGNA

Lasagne goes well with a mixed green salad! Argentina.

1 lb lasagna noodles
1 lb lean ground meat
1 cup cooked turkey meat, chopped
3 tbsp instant minced onion
1/4 tsp garlic powder
3 tbsp veg oil
1 15 oz can tomato paste
Salt, pepper to taste
1/4 tsp ground cumin
1 tsp oregano
1 tsp dry parsley
1 bay leaf
4 cups water put in blender with
1 cut up carrot and
1 tbsp chopped celery
1 tbsp honey
1 0.72 oz package low-fat Mozzarella cheese

Cook 12 lasagna noodles for 20 minutes in plenty of boiling salted water, in which 1 teaspoon oil has been added. Drain well. Spread them out on wax paper.

In large saucepan, fry ground meat until light brown. Save juices in small cup and put juices in freezer compartment. When grease hardens, throw grease away and add juice and turkey to ground meat.

Now, add minced onion, garlic powder and next 11 ingredients. Cover and simmer for one hour.

In 14x10x2-inch baking pan, arrange layers of noodles, meat tomato sauce, until you have four layers of noodles, ending with noodles, meat tomato sauce and cover with a layer of thinly sliced Mozzarella cheese.

Bake in 350° oven for 20 minutes.

Serves 8. Freezes well.

Tallarines

Noodles

2 cups unbleached flour
1 tsp salt
1/2 tsp baking powder
1/2 cup warm water
Corn starch

Sift dry ingredients. Add water, mix well. Roll very thin on a floured surface, keeping the shape rectangular.

Sprinkle dough with corn starch and fold in half. Roll again to original shape. Sprinkle with corn starch and fold once more. Do this about 3 or 4 times until you have about 12 lasagna noodles (10x3-inches).

CHANCHO ABOBADO

Roast Loin of Pork

Pork with a delicious barbecue flavor! Brazil.

7 lbs lean pork loin roast
1 tsp salt
1/4 tsp pepper
1 tsp cumin
1-1/2 tsp onion powder
1/2 cup catsup mixed with
1/3 cup brown sugar

Trim almost all fat from pork roast and rub with salt, pepper, cumin and onion powder. Place roast in an open roasting pan.

Heat oven to 350° and bake 2-1/2 hours then pour catsup and sugar mixture over pork roast and continue baking for 1/2 hr longer.

Loosen and remove backbone. Cut in thin slices. Serves 6.

CHULETAS DE CARNE A LA PARRILLA
Rib Steak, Grilled

The seasonings make this unusual. Paraguay.

1 6 rib standing beef roast
1/2 tsp pepper
1/2 tsp cumin
1 tsp garlic powder
1 tsp onion powder
Salt, to taste

Purchase a large 6 rib standing beef roast and have butcher cut it in 6 steaks, 1/2 inch thick. Season with next four ingredients.

Grill above hot coals to desired browness on one side, then turn over to brown on the other side. When ready, season with salt.

It goes well with corn on the cob, and a hearty green salad. Serves 6.

BISTES EMPANADOS
Breaded Round Steaks

Bolivia.

2 lbs round steak
Salt, pepper
1/4 tsp garlic powder
1 cup saltine cracker crumbs (put through blender)
Vegetable oil

Slice steak vertically into 6 portions. Pound each steak with small heavy mallet.

Season with salt, pepper, garlic powder and dip into cracker crumbs.

Fry in small amount of vegetable oil till golden brown on both sides.

Serve warm. Serves 6.

WALTER'S ANTICUCHOS
Peruvian Shish Kebab

The #1 favorite at the Janke-Grace households!

2 beef hearts
Salt, pepper
8 cloves garlic, minced
1 hot pepper
1 cup apple cider vinegar
2-1/2 tsp cumin powder
3 tbsp veg oil

Remove all fat and nerve endings from beef hearts and cut into inch cubes. Place in large bowl. Put next 6 ingredients in blender and blend for 1 minute. Pour over heart cubes, tossing well.

Refrigerate, covered, for 2 hours or longer.

Place 5 or 6 heart cubes on metal or wooden skewers. Lightly brush with vinegar mixture. Grill above hot coals, about 20 minutes, turning once and brushing cubes with enough vinegar-oil mixture to keep moist.

Serve with corn on the cob. Serves 6.

TAMALES MEJICANOS

Mexican Tamales

If you put too much hot pepper in the filling, these tamales will set your mouth on fire.

20 dry cornhusks
2-1/3 cups stone ground yellow corn meal
2-1/2 tsp baking powder
2 tsp salt
1/4 cup veg oil
1-1/2 cups seasoned chicken stock

Filling

2 tbsp veg oil
1 clove garlic, minced
1 small onion, chopped
1/2 tsp cumin powder
1 tsp fresh hot pepper, chopped
1 tbsp tomato sauce
1-1/2 cups cooked chicken meat, diced
1/4 cup Spanish peanuts
Salt, pepper to taste

When buying fresh corn, save cornhusks for wrapping tamales. These cornhusks will become very dry, but when you are ready to make the tamales, place cornhusks in a large pan of boiling water, cover pan, and turn heat off. Cornhusks should remain soaking in hot water for 1/2 hour. Drain them.

In medium size bowl, strain corn meal with baking powder and salt. Add oil, and with wooden spoon, begin to add and mix slowly the warm chicken stock. Continue to stir until it resembles a thick but slightly moist dough.

Filling. In small frying pan, heat oil; in it saute garlic, onion, cumin, hot pepper, for about 5 minutes. Add tomato sauce and cook 5 more minutes. Add chicken, peanuts, salt and pepper. Mix well.

Spread 2 tablespoons of the corn meal mixture on damp cornhusk and place 1 teaspoon of chicken filling in the center. Now, wrap cornhusk, envelope style, around tamale. Place tamales in a large strainer, one on top of the other, making sure that the ends of

cornhusk is under the tamale. Place this strainer over a very large pot of boiling water. Cover pan and simmer tamales for 1 hour.*

When done, place tamales on a large platter. Serve hot. 17 tamales. Freezes well.

* If you are familiar with a pressure cooker, you don't need the strainer. Tamales will cook in 2 cups of water for 15 minutes. Let the pressure go down normally.

FRIJOLES CON CHILI

Chili Con Carne

Good Mexican food with lots of protein for the day's activity.

1 lb Red Kidney beans
6 cups water
2 tbsp veg oil
1 cup chopped onion
1/2 lb ground beef
1/2 lb lean ground pork
1 4 oz can tomato sauce
2 tbsp bell pepper, chopped
2 tsp curry powder (hot)
1/4 tsp garlic powder
1 tsp chili pepper, chopped
1 tsp cumin
1 small leaf
Salt, pepper

Soak beans overnight in cold water. Drain. Cook beans in six cups cold water for about 2 hours. In large skillet, heat oil; in it saute onion until tender.

Add ground meats and fry till lightly brown. Throw grease away.

Add cooked beans with their liquid, tomato sauce and remaining ingredients. Heat to boiling, cover and simmer for 40 minutes, with occasional stirring.

Serves 10 to 12. Freezes well.

ESTOFADO GAUCHO

Argentinian Beef Stew

This is a very hearty stew from Argentine where beef is so plentiful.

1-1/2 lbs boneless beef
2 tbsp veg oil
1 onion, chopped
1/4 tsp each, pepper, curry powder, oregano, garlic powder, parsley flakes
Salt
1/2 cup water
1/2 cup red cooking wine
3 tbsp tomato sauce
4 med size carrots, sliced
4 med size potatoes, cubed
1 tbsp flour
1 tbsp corn starch

Cut beef into 1-/2 inch cubes.

In large skillet, heat oil, in it fry beef cubes until well browned. Add chopped onion and saute 5 more minutes. Add seasonings, water, wine, tomato sauce and simmer covered one hour. Add carrots and potatoes and cook covered until vegetables are done, about 20 minutes.

Mix flour, corn starch, and dissolve in water to make a smooth paste.

Add this paste to stew while stirring continuously. Simmer over low heat until thickened, about 5 minutes longer.

Serve with rice or mashed potatoes.

Serves 6 to 8. Freezes well.

SECO DE CORDERO

Lamb Stew

A stew with that unique Culantro flavor from Ecuador.

2 tbsp veg oil
6 lamb chops (trimmed of fat)
1 tsp hot pepper, chopped
1 onion, chopped
1/4 cup fresh culantro, chopped
1 large bell pepper, chopped
4 oz tomato sauce
Salt, pepper to taste
4 peeled and cubed potatoes
1 cup liquid from 1 lb can peas
1 can sweet peas (1 lb)
1 lime

In large skillet, heat oil; in it fry lamb chops. Add hot pepper, onion and saute till tender. Add culantro, bell pepper, tomato sauce, salt, pepper, potatoes and liquid from peas. Cover and simmer for 30 minutes or till lamb is tender.

Just before serving, add peas and juice of lime. Stir thoroughly. Serve with white rice. Serves 6 to 8. Freezes well.

ASADO CON BUDIN YORKSHIRE

Pot Roast with Yorkshire Pudding

This has long been a favorite with my father, Peru.

4 lb eye round roast
 (trimmed of fat)
1 tbsp cider vinegar
1 tbsp salt
1/4 tsp thyme
2 tbsp veg oil
1/2 bay leaf
1/4 tsp garlic powder
2 cups water
2 tbsp onion, chopped
4 tbsp flour
4 tbsp water

Early in the day rub roast with next three ingredients.

In large heavy skillet, heat oil. Fry roast till well browned on all sides. Add bay leaf, garlic powder, water and onion. Simmer covered for two hours or until very tender.

Skim fat from juices (if necessary, cool liquid, add one tray of ice cubes and fat will cling to cubes).

Make gravy by making a paste of flour and water. Add this paste to juices from pot roast, stirring well with wooden spoon till thickened.

Serves 10 to 12.

BUDIN YORKSHIRE

Yorkshire Pudding

4 tbsp veg oil
1/4 tsp onion powder
2 cups unbleached flour
1 tsp salt
5 eggs
2 cups nonfat milk

Heat oven to 450°. Put oil in large rectangular Pyrex dish with onion powder and place in hot oven to heat for 10 minutes.

In large bowl mix flour, salt, eggs, milk, and beat well for about 5 minutes until smooth.

Pour into dish with hot oil and bake at 450° for 15 minutes. Lower heat to 375° and bake 35 more minutes.

Cut in squares and serve around beef roast.

CARNE APIMENTADA

Pepper Steak

Panama.

1-1/2 lbs round steak
3 tbsp veg oil
1 large onion, sliced lengthwise
1 bell pepper, sliced in strips
1 tbsp tomato sauce
3 tbsp water
Salt
1/4 tsp oregano
1/4 tsp Cayenne pepper
1/2 cup French cut string beans, cooked
1/4 tsp freshly ground peppercorns

Slice meat, cutting across the grain, into very thin and short strips. In large skillet, heat oil; in it fry meat until nicely browned. Set aside. In same skillet saute onion and bell pepper for 5 minutes. Add tomato sauce, water, salt, oregano, Cayenne pepper and string beans. Simmer for 5 more minutes.

Add meat, ground peppercorns and mix thoroughly. Serve with white rice. Serves 6.

PEPIAN DE CHOCLO

Pork and Corn Casserole

A particularly good dish for a cold winter night. Peru.

1 lb pork, trimmed of all fat
2 1-lb bags frozen yellow corn kernels
1 cup water
2 tsp veg oil
1 onion, chopped
3 cloves garlic, minced
1 tbsp parsley, chopped
4 oz tomato sauce
1/4 tsp Cayenne pepper
1-1/2 tsp salt
1/4 tsp pepper
1/2 tsp oregano

Slice pork in very small cubes. Set aside. Cook corn kernels in 1 cup water for 15 minutes or until well done. Put corn and water in which it cooked in blender, and blend for 1 minute.

In large skillet, heat oil; in it fry pork, stirring with wooden spoon until pork is well done, for 20 minutes. Add onion, garlic, parsley, and saute 5 more minutes. Add tomato sauce, Cayenne pepper, salt, pepper, oregano, and cooked crushed corn. Cover and simmer for 10 more minutes, stirring occasionally.

Serve with white rice. Serves 6. Freezes well.

CARNE STROGANOFF

Beef Stroganoff

You should double the ingredients if you are expecting a large crowd. Brazil.

3 tbsp flour
1-1/2 lbs round steak
3 tbsp veg oil
1 onion, chopped
1 cup fresh mushrooms, sliced
1/4 tsp Worcestershire sauce
1 cup milk mixed with one tbsp vinegar
1 tsp salt
1/4 tsp pepper
1 tbsp fresh parsley, chopped

Pound flour into steak until very thin. Cut into 1/4 inch wide strips. In heavy skillet, heat oil; in it fry beef strips until well browned. Removed to bowl. In same skillet, add onion, mushrooms and a little more oil and saute for 5 minutes.

Return beef strips to skillet, stir in Worcestershire sauce, milk, and reheat to boiling. Season with salt and pepper.

Garnish with chopped parsley. Serve with noodles or white rice. Serves 6. Freezes well.

CHULETAS DE CHANCHO AL HORNO

Barbecued Pork Chops

Ecuador

6 lean pork chops
Salt, pepper
1/2 tsp garlic powder
1/2 tsp onion powder
1/2 tsp paprika
1/4 cup vinegar
1/2 cup catsup
1/4 cup brown sugar

Place lean pork chops on roasting rack. Season with salt, pepper, garlic powder, onion powder and paprika. Mix next three ingredients and baste chops.

Bake at 350° for 1-1/2 hrs. Serves 6.

CHULETAS DE CHANCHO A LA PARRILLA

Barbecued Country Style Pork Ribs

Brazil

4 lbs Country style pork ribs
1 cup water
1 cup catsup
1 tsp onion powder
1 tsp garlic powder
1/2 tsp cumin powder
1/3 cup brown sugar

Cook ribs in pressure cooker with 1 cup water for 20 minutes. Let the pressure go down normally. Save juice in refrigerator for soups, sauces. When fat hardens, throw fat away.

In large bowl, mix catsup with rest of ingredients. Place cooked ribs in this sauce and coat well. Barbecue for 20 minutes in closed barbecue grill so ribs won't burn.

Serves 5.

GOULASH HUNGARO

Hungarian Goulash

Uruguay

1-1/2 lbs round steak
3 tbsp veg oil
1 onion, chopped
2 carrots, scraped and sliced
2 tbsp chili powder
1 tsp salt
1/4 tsp pepper
4 oz tomato sauce
1 cup water

Cut steak into 1/4 inch wide strips and 1 inch long. In heavy skillet, heat oil; in it fry beef strips until well browned. Remove to bowl. In same skillet, add chopped onion and a little more oil (about 1 tablespoon) and saute for 5 minutes.

Return beef strips to skillet and add carrots. Season with chili powder, salt, pepper. Add tomato sauce and water. Cover and cook till meat is tender, about 30 minutes.

Serve with very small dumplings, rice or mashed potatoes. Serves 5. Freezes well.

PECHUGA DE POLLO CON PEREJIL

Chicken Breasts with Parsley

Chile.

6 chicken breasts (without skin and deboned)
1-1/2 tsp onion powder
1/4 tsp garlic powder
1 egg
1 tsp water
1 tbsp fresh parsley, chopped
Salt, pepper
1/2 cup veg oil

Cut chicken breasts in half, lengthwise. Season each one with onion and garlic powder. Beat egg with 1 tsp water, parsley, salt and pepper. Cover each breast with egg mixture.

In heavy skillet, heat oil; in it fry chicken breasts until a light golden color and breasts are cooked through, about 10 minutes on each side.

Serve with rice or mashed potatoes. Serves 6.

MATAMBRE

Stuffed Flank Steak

Many Argentinians eat this type of steak cold. Wrap steak roll tightly in aluminum foil and place in the refrigerator to cool. Unwrap and cut it into thin slices and serve with a hearty salad.

MEAT

2 tbsp veg oil
1-1/2 lbs flank steak
1-1/2 cups water

STUFFING

1/4 cup veg oil
1 onion, chopped fine
1 clove garlic, minced
1 carrot, chopped
1 tbsp parsley, chopped
1 tsp salt
Pepper
1-1/2 cups bread crumbs
1/4 cup white wine
1 egg
1/3 cup nonfat milk

MARINADE

1-1/2 tsp salt
2 cloves garlic, minced
1 bay leaf
1 tsp oregano
1 tsp fresh hot pepper, chopped
2 tbsp apple cider vinegar

GRAVY

1 tbsp flour
1 tbsp corn starch
1 tbsp veg oil
1/3 cup water

With a very sharp knife, slice steak horizontally, from one side to about 1/2 inch of the other side. With kitchen mallet, pound steak carefully, to thin it out. Place flank steak on a non-metallic container, and pour marinade over it. Let it stand for 1 or 2 hours at room temperature.

Stuffing. In large frying pan, heat oil; in it saute onion, garlic, carrot, parsley, for about 8 minutes. Turn heat off. Add salt, pepper, bread crumbs, wine, egg and milk. Mix well. Spread this filling over steak. Roll up tight, like jelly roll, starting at wide end. Fasten with strong wooden tooth picks, or tie with twine.

Meat. In large heavy pan, heat 2 tsp oil; in it brown steak roll on all sides. Add 1-1/2 cups water. Cover pan tightly, and simmer for 1 hour. Remove steak roll to platter and dispose of tooth picks or twine.

Gravy. Mix flour, corn starch, oil, and water, until smooth. Pour this paste to juices in pan, and cook by stirring with wooden spoon until gravy thickens. Simmer covered for 5 more minutes. With a sharp knife, slice meat roll into 1/4 inch slices. Pour gravy over individual servings.

Serves 5.

LOCRO

Corn and Beef Stew

The combination of corn and chunks of beef make this Peruvian dish worth trying.

- 1-1/2 lbs Butternut squash
- 1 tbsp veg oil
- 1 lb round steak, cubed
- 1 onion, chopped
- 3 cloves garlic, minced
- 1 tbsp parsley, chopped
- 1-1/2 cups water
- 1/4 tsp oregano
- Salt, pepper
- 1/4 tsp Cayenne pepper
- 4 oz tomato sauce
- 1 lb bag frozen yellow corn kernels
- 2 potatoes, peeled and cubed
- 1/4 tsp garlic powder
- 4 tbsp small curd cottage cheese

Peel squash and cut in small pieces. Set aside. In heavy skillet, heat oil; in it brown meat well. Add onion, garlic, parsley and simmer 10 more minutes. Add water and next 7 ingredients and the small pieces of squash. Cover and simmer for about half an hour or until meat is tender.

Add cottage cheese before serving and stir well. Serve with white rice. Serves 6.

CARNE MOLIDA CORDON BLEU

Cordon Bleu with Ground Beef

These delicious steaks stuffed with ham and cheese are served at the many continental restaurants of Lima.

- 1-1/2 lbs ground round
- 3 thin slices low-fat Mozzarella cheese
- 3 paper thin ham slices
- 1/2 cup bread crumbs (very fine and put in blender)
- Salt, pepper
- 1/4 tsp Cayenne pepper
- 1/4 tsp thyme
- 1/3 cup veg oil

Shape ground meat into 12 patties, resembling a T-bone steak. Pound each patty well. On each of 6 patties, place 1/2 slice cheese, 1/2 slice ham. Top each one, in sandwich fashion, with second patty half. Press edges together. Reshape to resemble a T-bone.

Coat with bread crumbs, which have been mixed with salt, pepper, Cayenne pepper and thyme. In large heavy skillet, heat oil; in it fry patties carefully, until well browned on both sides. Serves 6.

POLLO CORDON BLEU

Chicken Cordon Bleu

Exquisite!

6 chicken breasts skinned and boned
Salt, pepper
1/2 tsp onion powder
6 slices thin ham
6 slices thin low fat Mozzarella cheese
Flour
1 egg beaten with
1 tbsp water
Dry bread crumbs
Veg oil

Cut chicken breasts in half, lengthwise. Put each half inside a plastic lunch bag and pound with a cleaver until very thin. Season with salt, pepper and onion powder.

Place a slice of ham and cheese on 6 pieces of chicken and cover with remaining chicken breasts. Dust with flour carefully, dip in beaten egg and dust again with bread crumbs.

Heat oil; in it fry chicken until golden brown. Serves 6.

ARROZ CON POLLO #1

Chicken with Rice and culantro (Chinese parsley.)

Peru / It is always a success if you prepare this meal with cold cooked rice.

1 3 lb fryer, cut up
1/3 cup veg oil
2 large onions, chopped
6 cloves garlic, minced
1 cup fresh culantro leaves put through blender
4 oz tomato sauce
4 cups water
Salt, pepper
Hot pepper to taste
1 cup sweet peas (frozen)
5 cups cooked long grain rice (made early in the day or the day before) pg. 85
6 "Alfonso" olives

In large skillet fry cut up chicken with the oil until golden in color. Place chicken parts aside.

In same skillet saute onions and garlic until tender. Add culantro, tomato sauce, water, salt, pepper, hot pepper, sweet peas and chicken parts. Cover and simmer for 25 minutes.

Add cooked long grain rice and mix well. Cover again and simmer for 10 minutes, enough to warm rice.

Garnish with olives. Serves 6.

ARROZ CON POLLO #2

Chicken with Rice

We tried many rice dishes in Puerto Rico and this one is one of our favorites.

1 3 lb fryer, cut up
1/2 tsp oregano
1/4 tsp garlic powder
1 tbsp veg oil
1 tbsp vinegar
1 tbsp salt
1/4 tsp pepper
1/2 cup thick ham, cubed
3 tbsp veg oil
1 tsp cumin powder
1 tsp onion powder
1 8 oz can tomato sauce
1-1/2 cups water
1 small bell pepper, chopped
1 tsp dry parsley flakes
1/4 tsp thyme
4 cups cooked white rice (from day before) pg. 85
1 cup frozen sweet peas
10 pimento stuffed olives

Marinate cut up fryer with oregano, garlic, 1 tbsp veg oil, vinegar, salt, pepper. In large skillet, fry cubed ham. Add 3 tbsp veg oil, marinated chicken and fry till golden brown. Add cumin, onion powder, tomato sauce, water, bell pepper, parsley, thyme and season with salt to taste. Simmer covered for half an hour.

Add rice and mix well. Cover and simmer for about 10 minutes, enough to heat it through. Turn heat off. Cover again and let rice rest for 15 minutes.

Garnish with olives. Serves 6.

VATAPA

Bobby's Chicken Vatapa

One of our favorites from Brazil!

1 1-1/2 lb chicken
4 cups water
2 tbsp oil
1 8 oz can tomatoes
1 onion, chopped
1 tbsp fresh parsley, chopped
3 cloves garlic, minced
1 tbsp bell pepper, chopped
1/4 tsp each, oregano, thyme
Dash Cayenne pepper
Salt, pepper
1/4 cup shelled raw shrimp
3 cups chicken stock
1 cup bread crumbs
1 tbsp smooth peanut butter

Cook chicken in 4 cups water till tender, about one hour.

In large heavy skillet, heat oil; in it saute tomatoes, onion and rest of seasonings, for about 10 minutes. Add shrimp, chicken stock, bread crumbs, peanut butter and simmer for 15 minutes longer. Add deboned chicken.

Serve with white rice. Serves 6 to 8.

AJI DE GALLINA

Pepper Chicken with Walnuts

Peru / Served at large gatherings to celebrate the 28th of July—Peru's Independence Day.

1 large chicken
3 cups water
2 cups chicken stock, skimmed
1/3 cup oil
3 onions, chopped
3 cloves garlic, chopped
1 tsp parsley, chopped
6 slices wheat bread
1 cup non-fat milk
Salt, pepper, hot pepper, to taste
1/2 cup grated Parmesan cheese
1/2 cup chopped walnuts
2 large cooked potatoes, peeled and quartered

Boil chicken in water until tender. Drain and save chicken stock. Debone chicken and set aside.

In large pot, heat oil; in it saute onion, garlic and parsley till tender. Add bread which has been soaking in one cup milk and skimmed chicken stock. Stir well. Season with salt, pepper and hot pepper.

Add grated Parmesan cheese and walnuts. Heat thoroughly. Stir well. Add cooked potatoes and small chunks of deboned chicken.

Serves 6.

POLLO AL CURRY

Chicken Curry

Panama

1/2 cup flour
1 small fryer, cut-up
3 tbsp veg oil
1 large onion, chopped
3 cloves garlic, chopped
1 tsp ginger root, chopped
Salt, pepper
1-1/2 tsp curry powder
1/4 tsp thyme
1/4 tsp Cayenne pepper
1 cup celery, sliced
1/2 cup carrots, sliced
3 cups water
1 tsp lime juice

In large plastic bag place flour. Add cut-up chicken and shake bag to coat all pieces well.

In large skillet, heat oil; in it fry chicken till golden brown. Add onion, garlic and ginger. Saute until tender. Add salt, pepper, curry, thyme, cayenne pepper, celery, carrots and water, stirring with wooden spoon while mixture comes to a boil and thickens. Simmer, covered, for 20 minutes longer.

Just before serving time, add lime juice. Serve with white rice. Serves 6.

PAELLA

Puerto Rican Paella

Puerto Rico / We were introduced to this colorful dish at a seaside restaurant in Isla Verde.

1/3 cup veg oil
1 2-1/2 lb fryer, cut-up
Salt, pepper
2 large onions, chopped
1/4 tsp garlic powder
1 8 oz can tomato sauce
1/2 tsp oregano
1 cup frozen sweet peas
3 cups hot water
1/2 tsp dried saffron
1/2 cup shelled shrimp
1 Spanish sausage, sliced
4 cups cooked rice (made early in the day) pg. 85
1 4-oz can pimentos, cut into strips
8 olives

In large skillet, heat oil; in it fry chicken and brown well on all sides. Season with salt and pepper. Add onion, garlic and saute for 5 minutes.

Add tomato sauce, oregano, peas, and stir 1 minute. Add 3 cups hot water, saffron, shrimp, sausage. Cover and simmer 25 minutes longer.

Add rice and mix well. Turn heat off.

Arrange rice mixture on large platter. Garnish with pimento strips and olives. Serves 6 to 8.

POLLO CHINO CON HONGOS

Oriental Chicken

Lima has many good Chinese restaurants, and "Limenos" are very familiar with Chinese cooking. Peru.

3 tbsp veg oil
4 chicken breasts, skinned, boned and sliced thinly in 1-inch squares
1 tsp fresh ginger, chopped
3 cloves garlic, minced
3 bell peppers, diced
2 large onions, diced
1 cup sliced mushrooms
1 tsp fresh hot pepper, sliced
1-1/2 tsp corn starch, dissolved in
1/2 cup cold water
2 tbsp Soy sauce
1/2 cup bean sprouts

In heavy skillet, heat oil; in it stir fry sliced chicken pieces with wooden spoon, until chicken is cooked through, about 15 minutes. Add ginger, garlic and saute 5 more minutes. Add bell pepper, onion, mushrooms, hot pepper and stir fry 5 more minutes.

Add corn starch which has been dissolved in cold water and stir until liquid thickens.

Add Soy sauce and bean sprouts. Stir fry for 2 more minutes.

Serve with white rice. Serves 5.

ASOPAO DE POLLO CON TOSTONES

Soupy rice with chicken and plantains (Vilmita's favorite). Puerto Rico.

1 2-1/2 lb fryer, cut up
1/2 tsp oregano
1/4 tsp garlic powder
1 tbsp veg oil
1 tbsp lime juice
1 tbsp salt
1/4 tsp pepper
3 tbsp veg oil
1 tsp onion powder
2 8 oz cans tomato sauce
5 cups water
1 small bell pepper, chopped
1 cup sweet peas
1 tsp dry parsley flakes
1/4 tsp thyme
1 tbsp capers
2 tbsp Chinese parsley, chopped
5 cups cooked white rice (from day before) pg. 85
10 pimento stuffed olives
10 asparagus spears (canned & warm)

Marinate cut up fryer with oregano, garlic, 1 tbsp veg oil, lime juice, salt, pepper.

In large skillet, heat oil, add marinated chicken and fry till golden brown. Add onion powder, tomato sauce, water, bell pepper, sweet peas, parsley, thyme, capers and chinese parsley. Season with salt, to taste. Simmer, covered, for half an hour.

Add cooked rice and mix well. Cover and simmer for about 5 minutes till heated through. Turn heat off.

Cover again and let rice rest for 15 minutes.

Garnish with olives and asparagus spears. Serves 6 to 8.

Tostones
Fried Plantains

A must with Puerto Rican rice dishes.

3 plantains
1/2 cup veg oil
1/2 tsp salt

Peel plantains and save peelings. Cut into 1-inch thick slices.

In heavy frying pan, heat oil; in it saute plantain slices until soft and a very light golden color on both sides. Lift slices and place three at a time on one strip of the peeling. Place a second strip of peeling on top. Press hard with the palm of your hand, till slices are completely flat.

When all the slices have been flattened, saute these slices again in hot oil until a rich golden color on both sides. Transfer to platter.

Season with salt and serve warm. Serves 6.

ESCABECHE DE GALLINA
Marinated Chicken

Chile.

1 chicken cut-up into serving pieces
1-1/2 cups water
2 tbsps veg oil
2 onions, thinly sliced
1 bell pepper, cut in very thin rings
1 clove garlic, finely chopped
1 hot pepper, sliced fine
1/4 tsp oregano, thyme
1 bay leaf
1 tsp paprika
Salt, pepper
1/2 cup apple cider vinegar
Lettuce leaves
Green pitted olives
1 Hard boiled egg

Place cut-up chicken in large pot with water. Cover, let it come to a boil and simmer till tender, about one hour. Save liquid for making soup.

In large frying pan heat oil, in it fry onions, bell pepper, garlic, hot pepper, oregano, thyme, bay leaf, paprika, till tender. Add salt, pepper and vinegar allowing it all to come to a boil. Immediately pour this onion mixture over cooked chicken. (Debone chicken, before pouring onion-vinegar mixture, if desired). Refrigerate.

Garnish platter with lettuce leaves, olives and egg wedges. Serves 6.

POLLO GUISADO CON VEGETALES

Chicken Vegetable Stew

Uruguayans are known for their well seasoned dishes.

2 tbsp flour
2 tsp salt
1/4 tsp pepper
1 2-1/2 lb fryer, cut up
1/4 cup olive oil
3/4 cup onions, chopped
1/4 tsp garlic powder
2 tbsp parsley, chopped
2 tbsp bell pepper, chopped
1 8 oz can tomato sauce
1 carrot, sliced thin
1 potato, cubed
1/4 tsp oregano
1/4 tsp thyme
1 bay leaf
1/4 tsp basil
1/2 cup red wine
1 cup orange juice
1 cup cooked peas

In paper bag, combine flour with salt and pepper. Add chicken pieces and shake to coat all pieces well. In large heavy skillet, heat oil; add chicken pieces and brown well on both sides. Remove them from skillet to platter.

To remaining drippings in skillet, add onion, garlic, parsley and bell pepper. Saute until tender.

Add tomato sauce, carrot, potato and seasonings. Add chicken pieces, red wine and orange juice. Bring to a boil and simmer covered 30 minutes.

Garnish with peas. Serve with white rice. Serves 8. Freezes well.

POLLO FRITO AL HORNO

Baked Tasty Chicken

Very easy to make! Haiti.

1 2-1/2 lb fryer, cut-up
2 tbsp veg oil
1/4 tsp each, garlic powder, cumin powder, onion powder, pepper, Cayenne pepper
1/2 tsp salt
1/2 cup fine saltine cracker crumbs (put in blender for 1/2 minute)

Rub oil and seasonings all over fryer parts.

Coat all chicken parts with cracker crumbs.

Place chicken pieces in large rectangular Pyrex dish. Bake in 375° oven for 1 hour.

Serves 5.

TORTA DE GALLINA TIJUCA

Chicken Pie

Brazil.

1 2-1/2 lb fryer
6 cups water
1 tbsp salt
1/4 tsp pepper
1 large onion, cut up
1/4 tsp each, thyme, oregano, basil, Cayenne pepper
3 medium potatoes, cubed
3 carrots, sliced
2 tbsp bell pepper, chopped
1/2 cup celery, sliced
1 cup frozen peas
2 tbsp corn starch
2 tbsp flour
1/2 cup water
1 tsp lime juice

Cook fryer in 6 cups water with salt, pepper, onion, thyme, oregano, basil and Cayenne pepper until tender, about one hour. Remove fryer to platter and debone.

Cook potatoes, carrots, bell pepper, celery and peas in one cup of the chicken broth. When tender, add to remaining broth.

Now, make a smooth paste with corn starch, flour and water. Add slowly to chicken broth and stir continuously until thickened. Add deboned chicken, and lime juice and mix well.

Pour mixture into 2 9-inch pie plates. Cover with pie crust. Bake in 425° oven for about 20 minutes, or until nicely browned.

Serves 8 to 10.

PASTA PARA PASTEL

Pie Crust (Enough for 2 pie crusts)

2 cups flour
1 tsp salt
10 tbsp margarine
2/3 cup cold non-fat milk

Sift flour with salt. Cut in margarine with 2 knives until mixture resembles rice grains. Add milk all at once, stirring quickly with a fork until dough just stiffens.

Divide dough in half. Roll each one into a ball. Roll each one between two pieces of wax paper, until it is of desired size. Peel away wax paper. Prick it in several places to allow steam to escape and place crust on top of pie.

POLLO COLOMBIANO

Colombian Style Chicken

5 tbsp flour
2 tsp salt
1/4 tsp pepper
1 2-1/2 lb fryer, cut-up
1/4 cup veg oil
3/4 cup onions, chopped
3 cloves garlic, minced
2 tbsp each, parsley, bell pepper, chopped
1/2 cup fresh mushrooms, sliced
1 16 oz can tomatoes
1 carrot, sliced fine
1 cup sweet peas
1/4 tsp each, oregano, thyme, basil
1/2 cup red table wine
6 pimento-stuffed olives

In paper bag, combine flour with salt and pepper. Add chicken pieces and shake to coat all pieces well. In large skillet, heat oil; in it fry chicken pieces until golden brown. Remove chicken from skillet to platter.

To remaining drippings in skillet, add chopped onion, garlic, parsley, bell pepper, and mushrooms. Saute until tender. Add tomatoes, carrots, peas and rest of seasonings. Add chicken pieces, red wine. Stir and bring to a boil and simmer covered for 15 minutes.

Uncover, and simmer 15 minutes longer.

Serve on large platter. Garnish with olives. Serve with white rice. Serves 6 to 8.

PANQUEQUES DE ESPARRAGO Y POLLO

Crepes—Filled with Asparagus and Chicken

A big success at luncheons. Guatemala.

Batter
3/4 cups flour
1/4 tsp salt
2 eggs
1 tbsp veg oil
1-1/2 cups milk

Filling
2 cups white sauce (see below)
1/2 cup asparagus liquid
1/2 tsp onion powder
1 tsp dry parsley (optional)
12 very thin slices of cooked chicken breasts
36 tender asparagus spears
Evaporated skimmed milk
2 tbsp Parmesan cheese

Sift flour and salt into a bowl. Add eggs and oil; add milk slowly beating continuously with electric beater until smooth. Cover and place in refrigerator for about 2 hours.

Make white sauce. Add to it liquid from asparagus, onion powder and parsley. Set aside.

For crepes, heat 1 tsp veg oil in 7" skillet. Pour in about 2 tbsp batter, tilt pan so the batter covers it entirely. When crepes are set, loosen with spatula and turn over for just a second. Makes about 12 crepes.

Lay a thin slice of cooked chicken and 3 asparagus spears on each crepe. Spread a spoonful of white sauce in center and roll up.

Arrange crepes side by side in 2 glass rectangular baking dishes and cover with remaining white sauce thinned with evaporated milk. Sprinkle with Parmesan cheese and broil for a few minutes.

Serve hot. Serves 6.

Salsa Blanca Basica

Basic White Sauce

2 tbsp veg oil
2 tbsp flour
2 cups hot water mixed with
2/3 cup powdered milk
Salt, pepper to taste
1/4 tsp onion powder

In medium saucepan, heat oil; add flour and stir well. Add rest of ingredients, stirring continuously until thickened. Bring to a boil and simmer for 8 minutes.

PASTEL DE ESPINACA

Spinach, Cheese and Pork Souffle

Peru / This souffle is often served at large gatherings.

2 lbs raw frozen spinach
2 eggs
2/3 cup Parmesan cheese
1 tsp salt
1/2 lb pork sausage
2 cups nonfat milk
3 bread slices
3 tbsp veg oil
1 onion, chopped
2 cloves garlic, minced
1/2 tsp. oregano
1 tbsp tomato sauce
1/4 tsp pepper
1 hard boiled egg

Place frozen spinach in large pan without water. Cover and simmer over very low heat until tender, about 25 minutes.

Put spinach in blender with eggs, Parmesan cheese, salt, and blend 2 seconds.

In medium size skillet, fry pork sausage till thoroughly done. Throw grease away. Mix sausage with milk and bread. Set aside.

In large skillet, heat oil; in it saute onion, garlic, oregano, till tender. Add tomato sauce, pepper, cooked spinach and sausage meat mixture. Mix well and pour half of this mixture in greased 8-inch square pan.

Place hard boiled egg slices on top and cover with remaining spinach meat mixture. Sprinkle with remaining Parmesan cheese and bake in 350° oven for 20 minutes or until a nice golden color.

Cut in squares. Serves 8.

LENTEJAS CON JAMON

Lentils with Ham

Peru / Lentils have always been a big treat at my house!

1/2 lb dried lentils
2 tsp salt
2 tbsp veg oil
1/2 cup onion, chopped
1 clove garlic, minced
3 tbsp tomato sauce
1/2 tsp oregano
1/4 tsp Cayenne pepper
1/2 lb ham, cubed
2 tbsp parsley, chopped

Wash lentils, drain, cover with fresh cold water, add salt. Let it all come to a boil and simmer covered for 30 minutes.

In large skillet, heat oil, in it saute onion and garlic till tender. Add lentils with their cooking water, tomato sauce, oregano, Cayenne pepper and ham. Simmer 25 minutes longer.

Garnish with parsley. Serve with white rice. Serves 6. Freezes well.

PIMIENTONES RELLENOS
Stuffed Peppers

Nicaragua.

6 medium-sized green peppers
1 cup boiling water
1/2 tsp salt
2 cups left over meat-tomato sauce
1 cup cold cooked rice
3/4 cup breadcrumbs, mixed with two teaspoons Parmesan cheese
2 tbsp margarine

Wash peppers, cut off the tops, and remove seeds. Parboil peppers 5 minutes in boiling water with 1/2 teaspoon salt. Remove from water and drain.

Place peppers in an oiled baking dish. Mix meat-tomato sauce with cooked rice and stuff peppers. Sprinkle breadcrumb mixture on top of each pepper and dot with margarine.

If there is any left over sauce and rice, place this and the water in which the bellpeppers cooked in the blender and blend one second. Pour around bellpeppers.

Bake in a preheated oven at 350°F for 50 minutes, or until crumbs are golden brown. Serves 6.

REPOLLITOS AL HORNO
Stuffed Cabbage Leaves

With meat-tomato sauce. Costa Rica.

1 head of cabbage, 2 lbs
1/2 lb ground beef
16 oz low fat cottage cheese
1/4 tsp garlic powder
1 tsp salt
1/4 tsp pepper
1 egg
2 bread slices, crumbled
1/4 cup tomato juice
1/2 cup sliced carrots
1 onion, sliced
1 tbsp veg oil

Cover cabbage with boiling water and let stand covered for 10 minutes. Separate leaves carefully by removing core.

Steam 1/2 lb ground beef in covered pan. When cooked, combine with cottage cheese, garlic, salt, pepper, egg, bread, tomato juice.

Place 2 tablespoons of this mixture on each leaf and fold up envelope style.

Place carrots and onions with 1 tablespoon vegetable oil in 14 x 10 x 2 aluminum baking pan. Lay cabbage rolls, flap down, on top. Cover with meat tomato sauce.

Place, covered, in 350° oven for 1 hour. Serves 6.

Salsa De Carne Con Tomate
Meat Tomato Sauce

1/2 lb ground meat
1 onion, chopped
1/4 tsp each, thyme, garlic powder, basil
1/2 tsp oregano
1 tsp salt
4 oz tomato sauce
1/2 cup cooking wine
1 tsp sugar

In heavy skillet, fry ground meat till brown. Throw grease away. Add onion, saute till tender. Add rest of ingredients and simmer for 20 minutes longer. This sauce freezes well.

CAU-CAU A LA LIMEÑA
Tripe, Peruvian Style

Peru / Tripe is served in many native restaurants.

2 lbs fresh honeycombe tripe
3 sprigs green celery leaves
1 bay leaf
1/4 tsp thyme, pepper
1 tsp salt
3 cups water
3 tbsp veg oil
1/2 cup chopped onions
3 cloves garlic, minced
4 potatoes, cubed
1 pkg frozen peas (1 lb)
1 tsp curry powder
Cayenne pepper, to taste
1/2 cup fresh parsley, chopped

Place tripe in large pan with next 5 ingredients. Cover and cook over medium heat 2 hours or until very tender. Save liquid in freezing compartment of refrigerator. Cut tripe into thin strips and these into cubes.

In heavy skillet heat oil; in it saute onions and garlic until tender. Add cubed tripe, 2 cups liquid (without grease), potatoes, peas and curry powder. Cover, bring to a boil and simmer for half an hour.

Season with Cayenne pepper. Garnish with parsley. Serve with white rice. Serves 6. Freezes well.

MONDONGUITO ITALIANO

Tripe Italian Style

Argentina / very tasty!

1-1/2 lbs fresh honeycombe tripe
3 cups water
1 sprig celery leaves
1 branch parsley
1/3 cup veg oil
1 onion, chopped
3 cloves garlic, minced
1 tbsp parsley, chopped
5 mushrooms, sliced
3 tbsp tomato paste
1/2 cup Burgundy wine
2 carrots, sliced
3 large potatoes, cubed
Salt, pepper, to taste
Cayenne pepper
1/2 cup grated Parmesan cheese

Place tripe in large pan with water and next two ingredients. Cover and cook 2 hours or until very tender. (This time can be greatly reduced if cooked in a pressure cooker). Save liquid in freezing compartment of refrigerator. Cut tripe into thin strips.

In heavy skillet, heat oil; in it saute onion, garlic, parsley, mushrooms, until tender. Add tripe strips, 2 cups liquid in which tripe was cooked (without grease), tomato paste, wine, carrots, potatoes, season with salt, pepper, Cayenne pepper, to taste. Simmer covered for half an hour, or until vegetables are tender.

Garnish with Parmesan cheese. Serves 6. Freezes well.

COL CON JAMON Y POLLO

Cabbage Mandarin

Rio De Janeiro Brazil / A delightful union of ham and chicken.

1 2-1/2 lb chicken
5 cups water
1 tbsp dry onion flakes
Salt, pepper to taste
1 medium size carrot
1 small head cabbage
12 ham slices, sliced very thin
1 tbsp corn starch
Soy sauce

In large pan place chicken with next four ingredients. Let it all come to a boil. Simmer one hour. Lift chicken and set aside. Slice when lukewarm.

Place head of cabbage in boiling chicken stock and simmer for 20 minutes. Lift cabbage and set aside. With sharp knife cut around cabbage core so that leaves will come loose easily.

In large rectangular Pyrex dish place a folded cabbage leaf, next to it a slice of cooked chicken, folded cabbage leaf, ham slice, beginning and ending with cabbage leaves.

Dissolve corn starch in small amount of lukewarm chicken stock, add 1-1/2 cups of chicken stock, and season with Soy sauce. Let it come to a boil and simmer till stock is clear, about 5 minutes. Pour on top of cabbage leaf arrangement.

Keep in lukewarm oven till ready to serve. Serve with pork fried rice or plain white rice. Serves 6.

WANTAN FRITO
Fried Wantan

Panama / the thinner the skin, the crispier it will be.

2 cups flour
1 tsp salt
1-1/2 tsp baking powder
1/3 cup warm water
[corn starch]
1 beaten egg white

Sift dry ingredients. Add water, mixing well. Roll very thin, by turning dough onto a floured surface, kneading well. Roll dough into a rectangle and sprinkle corn starch liberally over it. Then fold in half. Roll again. Sprinkle with more corn starch once again and proceed till you have accumulated several layers of thin skins. Corn starch will keep skins from sticking to each other.

Cut Wantan skins 5x6-inches. Fill by placing about 1/2 a teaspoon of filling in center of skin. Fold one corner over filling to meet the opposite corner, sealing with very small amount of egg white. Turn two remaining corners under and over so that all corners meet at the center, sealing them with one drop of beaten egg white.

Fry in hot deep oil, till crisp and golden in color.

Serve with sweet and sour sauce. About 25 skins.

Filling
1/2 cup cooked hot sausage meat
1/2 tsp ginger root, chopped
1/2 tsp garlic, chopped

Mix all ingredients and fill Wantan skins with 1/2 teaspoon of this filling.

Sweet and Sour Sauce
2 tbsp veg oil
1/4 tsp garlic, chopped fine
1/4 tsp ginger chopped fine
Pinch Cayenne pepper
2 tbsp white vinegar
5 tbsp sugar
1/2 tsp Soy sauce
1-1/2 tsp corn starch
10 tbsp water
1 scallion, chopped

In small pan, heat oil; in it saute garlic, ginger, Cayenne pepper, for 1/2 minute. Add vinegar, sugar, Soy sauce and corn starch, which has been diluted in water. Let it all come to a boil and simmer for 3 minutes. Garnish with chopped scallions.

BISTE CON HONGOS Y FREJOLITOS CHINOS

Steak with Mushrooms, Bean Sprouts

Paraguay.

Sprouts

If fresh bean sprouts are desired, sprout your own 6 days before preparing this meal. Place 1 cup Mung or soy beans inside a clean empty 1 gallon plastic (milk) container with top part cut off. Fill with water and soak beans overnight, about 10 hours. Pour off water. Place container on its side until beans sprout. Keep moist by pouring lukewarm water over the beans twice a day. Drain well. Beans should be kept damp, not wet.

When sprouts are ready, wash and remove skins. Use as needed. (Yields approximately 3 cups of sprouts)

2 tbsp veg oil
1-1/2 lbs flank steak
2 cloves garlic, chopped
1 onion, sliced thin lengthwise
1 tsp ginger root, chopped fine
1 cup fresh mushrooms, sliced thin
2 tbsp Soy sauce
1/2 cup water mixed with 1-1/2 tsp corn starch
3 cups bean sprouts
Salt, pepper

Steak

Slice flank steak paper-thin, diagonally across grain. In heavy skillet, heat oil; in it fry meat strips till well done on all sides. Set aside.

To same frying pan, add garlic, onion, ginger root, mushrooms, and saute until tender. Add Soy sauce, water paste and bring to a boil. Simmer for 5 minutes.

Add fried meat, bean sprouts. Season with salt, pepper.

Serve with white rice. Serves 6.

BISTE JAPONES SALTADO CON VERDURAS

Sukiyaki–Japanese sliced steak with vegetables

In downtown Rio de Janeiro, we tasted this delicious version of "Sukiyaki."

1 lb sirloin steak
2 tbsp veg oil
2 cloves garlic, minced
1 tsp fresh ginger root, chopped fine
1-1/2 tsp corn starch, mixed with 1 cup cold water
1 large onion, sliced in thin strips
1/2 lb fresh spinach, washed
2 scallions, cut in 2" pieces
3 medium size carrots, cooked and sliced diagonally
1 egg
Soy sauce
Salt, pepper, to taste
Cayenne pepper

Slice steak, cutting across the grain, into paper thin square shaped strips. In medium size iron skillet, heat oil; in it saute garlic and ginger for about 5 minutes. Add sirloin strips and brown well. Add corn starch, which has been dissolved in the water. Use wooden spoon to stir the food while it cooks. Let it all come to a boil. Simmer for 5 minutes. Transfer meat and juices to large iron skillet and place skillet in warm oven.

In medium size iron skillet, add more vegetable oil, as needed, and saute onion for 5 minutes. Lift onions and place next to beef strips. Snip spinach and simmer in same skillet for about 5 minutes, stirring well. Lift and place next to onions.

Saute scallions for 5 minutes, lift and place next to spinach. Place cooked carrots next to scallions. Break egg and drop it in center of large skillet with all the meat and vegetables around it. Cover skillet.

Place over medium heat and simmer till egg is set, about 2 more minutes. Season with salt, pepper, Soy sauce and Cayenne pepper.

Serve with white rice. Serves 5.

TORTILLA SABROSA

Savory Omelet

Jamaica

2 tbsp veg oil
1 onion, chopped
2 tbsp tomato sauce
1 tsp dry bell pepper
3 tbsp parsley, chopped
1/2 cup thinly sliced cooked chicken
1/4 tsp Cayenne pepper
1 tsp salt
4 eggs, beaten slightly

In heavy skillet, heat oil; in it saute onion, till tender. Add tomato sauce, bell pepper, parsley, chicken, pepper, salt, and simmer for 5 minutes.

Pour beaten eggs on top. Cover. Simmer over very low heat until eggs are set, about 5 more minutes. Cut omelet into pie shaped servings. Serves 6.

PANAMITOS GUISADOS

Creole White Navy Beans

Peru / very tasty.

1 lb Michigan Navy Beans (white)
1 piece smoked pork hock
3 tbsp veg oil
1 onion, chopped
3 cloves garlic, minced
1 tbsp parsley, chopped
1 tbsp bell pepper, chopped
1/2 tsp oregano
2 large tomatoes, chopped
Salt, pepper

Place beans in large pan and cover with double amount of water for six hours.

Drain. Cook in pressure cooker with pork hock and water, about one inch above the bean line, for 20 minutes. Let the pressure go down normally.

In another pan, heat oil, in it saute next six ingredients until tender. Add cooked beans and season with salt and pepper.

Serve with white rice. Serves 8. Freezes well.

FRIJOLES NEGROS GUISADOS

Creole Black Turtle Beans

Brazil / A must in Rio De Janeiro!

1 lb Black Turtle Beans
Water
1 piece smoked pork hock
3 tbsp veg oil
1 onion, chopped
3 cloves garlic, minced
1 tbsp parsley, chopped
1 tbsp bell pepper, chopped
1/2 tsp oregano
1 bay leaf
2 large tomatoes, chopped
Salt, pepper

Place beans in large pan and cover with double amount of water for six hours or overnight.

Drain. Cook in pressure cooker with pork hock and water, about two inches above the bean line, for 30 minutes. Let pressure go down normally.

In another pan, heat oil, in it saute next seven ingredients. Add cooked beans and season with salt and pepper. Serve with white rice.

Serves 8.

PAPAS RELLENAS

Stuffed Potatoes

Peru / These can be found at many native fairs.

9 med size potatoes
2 eggs
1 tbsp salt

Cook potatoes in small amount of water till well done.

Mash without water, adding eggs and salt. Mix thoroughly. Divide mashed potatoes into egg sized balls on wax paper. Flatten on palm of hand and place 1 teaspoon of filling in center. Close and form into egg shaped balls.

Dip balls into batter and fry until a golden color. Serves 6.

Filling

2 tbsp veg oil
2 tbsp onion, chopped
1 clove garlic, minced
1 tbsp tomato sauce
1/2 tsp cumin powder
1 cup cooked ground beef
Salt, pepper
1 hard boiled egg, cut in wedges
1 tbsp raisins
4 pitted olives, cut-up

In medium size skillet heat oil, in it saute onion and garlic till tender. Add tomato sauce, cumin, ground beef, salt, pepper. Place filling in center of potato mixture, adding a small sliver of egg, raisin, olive. Close and proceed as above.

Batter for Potatoes

1 cup flour mixed with
  1-1/2 cups water
1 tsp baking powder
1 tsp salt

Mix all ingredients and use to dip all potato balls in this mixture before frying.

PALTAS RELLENAS CON POLLO

Stuffed Avocados with Chicken

In Bolivia avocados are a treat.

1-1/2 cups diced chicken
1/2 cup mayonnaise
1/2 tsp salt
1/4 tsp pepper
1 tbsp lemon juice
1/3 cup walnuts, chopped
3 avocados

Combine chicken with next 5 ingredients. Cut avocados in half, lengthwise. Remove pit. Fill each half with chicken mixture. Refrigerate.

Serves 6.

ZAPALLITO RELLENO AL HORNO

Baked Stuffed Zucchini

with that good Italian flavor! Argentina.

1 large zucchini
2 cups meat-tomato sauce
1/3 cup Parmesan cheese
1/2 cup low-fat Mozzarella cheese, shredded

Wash zucchini and cut in half lengthwise. Scoop out the pulp, and dice (cut in small pieces.) Mix meat-tomato sauce with diced zucchini. Stuff zucchini shells with this mixture. Sprinkle with cheeses.

Bake in a 350° oven for 1 hour. Transfer to a large platter. Serves 6.

Rice Cookery

ARROZ FRITO CON POLLO Y FREJOLITOS CHINOS

Chicken Fried Rice and Bean Sprouts

Panama.

1 tbsp veg oil
2 eggs
3 cups cooked white rice (cold)
2 tbsp Soy sauce
1 cup cooked chicken breast, cubed
4 tbsp scallions, chopped
1 cup fresh bean sprouts

In large skillet, heat oil. Add slightly beaten eggs.

When set, place scrambled eggs in pyrex dish, in oven, to keep warm. In same skillet, place cooked cold rice and stir fry with Soy sauce, until warmed through. Add cubed chicken, scallions, bean sprouts and mix well until very warm.

Garnish with the scrambled eggs. Serves 6.

ARROZ A LA GRIEGA

Greek Rice

In downtown Rio de Janeiro we had this type of rice served with fish from Bahia.

3 cups cooked white rice (cooked early in the day)
1 cup cooked chopped spinach
1/2 cup cooked chopped carrots
1/4 cup cooked peas
Salt, pepper to taste

Place all ingredients in large frying pan over medium heat. Stir with wooden spoon until all ingredients are heated through. Serves 6.

ARROZ FRITO CON CURRY

Curried Fried Rice

With bits of chicken

2 tbsp veg oil
1 cup onion, chopped
1 cup celery, chopped
1 tbsp curry powder
1 cup cubed cooked chicken
Salt, pepper
4 cups cooked white rice (made early in the day)
1 omelette (egg beaten with
1 tbsp water and fried in
1 tsp veg oil)

In large skillet, heat oil; in it saute onion and celery until tender. Add curry, cooked chicken, salt, pepper and rice. Stir and fry till piping hot.

Garnish with strips of omelette. Serves 6.

TORTILLA DE ARROZ

Japanese Rice Omelet

Brazil.

2 tbsp veg oil
1/2 onion, chopped
2 tbsp bell pepper, chopped
1 clove garlic, chopped
2 tbsp tomato sauce
1 cup cold cooked rice
1-1/2 tsp salt
3 eggs
1/4 tsp hot sauce
3 tbsp water
Salt, pepper
1 tbsp veg oil

In medium size pan, heat oil; in it saute onion, bell pepper, and garlic for 10 minutes. Add tomato sauce, rice, salt and mix well. Stir till heated through. Turn heat off.

Leave rice covered in pan for 10 minutes until ready to serve.

Omelet

Mix eggs with hot sauce, water. Season with salt, pepper. In large skillet, heat oil; in it pour egg mixture. Let it spread all over skillet. Simmer under very low heat until eggs are set.

Transfer to large platter. Fill omelet with rice and close as much as omelet will allow. Serves 6.

ARROZ FRITO CON CHANCHO

Pork Fried Rice

Panama.

2 tbsp veg oil
1 clove garlic, minced
1 onion, chopped
2 scallions, chopped
2 eggs, beaten slightly
3 cups cooked cold white rice
Soy sauce
1 lb cooked diced pork (lean)
1/2 cup fresh bean sprouts
Salt, pepper
Chopped scallions

In large skillet, heat oil; in it saute garlic, onion and scallions until tender.

Add beaten eggs and scramble. Add cooked rice. Stir till heated through. Add Soy sauce, pork, bean sprouts, salt, pepper. Fry about one minute longer.

Serve hot. Garnish with fresh chopped scallions. Serves 6.

ARROZ FRITO CON POLLO

Chicken Fried Rice

Brazil.

2 tbsp veg oil
1/4 tsp garlic powder
2 onions, chopped
1 cup celery, chopped
Salt, pepper
2 eggs, beaten
Soy sauce (about 1 tbsp)
3 cups cooked white rice (made early in the day)
1 cup cubed chicken meat
6 chopped scallions

In heavy skillet, heat oil; in it saute garlic, onions, celery, salt and pepper for about 5 minutes. Add beaten eggs and stir. Add Soy sauce, cooked rice and chicken. Fry till heated throughout.

Mix well. Garnish with chopped scallions. Serves 6.

ARROZ BLANCO BASICO

Basic White Rice

Peru / You can double the ingredients if you are planning other rice dishes later in the week.

2-1/2 tbsp veg oil
1 tsp onion powder
1/4 tsp garlic powder
2 cups long grain white rice (or med. grain)
4 cups hot water
1-1/2 tsp salt

In medium pan, heat oil; add onion powder, garlic powder and rice. Stir twice. Add hot water, salt and let it all come to a full boil. Cover and simmer for 20 minutes without stirring.

Uncover, give rice a full turn and cover again. Turn heat off.

Leave resting for 15 minutes before serving. Makes about 5 cups cooked rice. Serves 6.

ARROZ TAPADO

Rice and Blackeyed Peas

In tomato sauce, Peru.

1/2 lb bag blackeyed peas
4 cups cooked white rice
meat-tomato sauce, pg. 48
Parmesan cheese

Soak blackeyed peas in cold water half an hour before cooking time.

Drain. Cover with fresh water and cook covered for 1 hour, or until tender.

Drain. Place layer of cooked rice in 9-inch round Pyrex plate, then layer of cooked peas, another of rice, and so on, ending with a layer of rice. Press with fingers all around and turn over on serving platter.

Cover with meat-tomato sauce and garnish with Parmesan cheese. This dish can be shaped in a small Pyrex cup and turned over on individual serving plates. Serves 6.

Vegetables

ALCACHOFAS JUANITA

Peru / My mom made artichoke eating a memorable occasion!

6 artichokes
1 tsp salt
boiling water
1/2 cup vinegar
1/3 cup veg oil
1-1/2 tsp salt (or to taste)

Wash artichokes and drain. Place them in large pan with salt and enough boiling water to cover them. Cover and cook 35 to 40 minutes. (If using pressure cooker, place artichokes inside pressure cooker, add 1/2 cup water, cover and cook with 15 lbs pressure for 10 minutes. Let pressure go down normally.)

Drain off water. Place artichokes on serving dish.

Mix vinegar, oil and salt to taste. Distribute this mixture in 6 pyrex cups.

To eat artichoke, dip the stem end into vinegar mixture, then bite off the stem part between the teeth. Discard the petals. Scrape the heart of the artichoke with a spoon and discard hairy exterior. Cut the heart of the artichoke in quarters and dip in the vinegar mixture.

Serves 6.

PAPAS A LA CACEROLA

Escalloped Potatoes

Chile.

3 tbsp veg oil
1 small onion, chopped
2 tbsp flour
Salt, pepper, to taste
1 tsp basil
2-1/2 cups low fat milk
6 cups sliced potatoes

In large pan, heat oil; in it saute onion until tender, about 5 minutes. Add flour, salt, pepper, basil and mix well with wooden spoon. Add milk slowly and stir over medium heat until liquid begins to thicken. Add sliced potatoes, stirring until the sauce begins to boil. Lower heat and simmer covered for 30 minutes.

Turn potatoes with sauce into a 2 qt rectangular shallow Pyrex dish. Bake at 350° for about 20 more minutes.

Serves 6.

PICANTE DE PAPAS

Spicy Potatoes

Lots of these potatoes are eaten in the sierras of Peru.

4 large potatoes
2 tbsp veg oil
1 onion, chopped
2 cloves garlic, minced
2 tbsp tomato sauce
1 tsp hot pepper, chopped
1/2 tsp oregano
Salt, pepper
1 cup water
1/4 cup evaporated skimmed milk
1 tbsp parsley, chopped

Peel potatoes and cut in small cubes. In heavy skillet heat oil; in it saute onion with garlic until tender. Add tomato sauce, hot pepper, oregano, salt, pepper, water and cubed potatoes. Cook till potatoes are tender.

Just before serving add milk and mix well. Garnish with parsley. Serves 6.

COUVE MINEIRA

Minas Gerais Cabbage

Brazil.

2 tbsp veg oil
2 tbsp onion, chopped
1/4 tsp garlic powder
1 tbsp tomato sauce
1/4 tsp thyme
1/2 cup water
1 med cabbage, finely shredded
Salt, pepper

In medium size pan, heat oil; in it saute onion until tender. Add garlic, tomato sauce, thyme, water and finely shredded cabbage. Let it come to a full boil.

Cover and simmer until just tender, about 12 minutes. Season with salt, pepper. Serves 6.

VAINITAS A LA CASERA

Creole Green Beans

Uruguay.

1-1/2 lbs green beans
2 tbsp veg oil
1 onion, chopped
1 clove garlic minced
1/2 cup water
1 tsp salt
Pepper
1 tsp paprika
2 tbsp margarine

Wash beans (stringless type), and cut stems off. Leave whole.

In large pan, heat oil; in it saute onion, garlic, until tender. Add beans, water, and cover tightly. Cook over medium heat for about 10 minutes.

Turn heat off and leave pan covered for another 15 minutes so that beans will continue to cook in their own steam. Water should have evaporated by now. Add salt, pepper, paprika, and margarine. Stir beans carefully until margarine has melted.

Serves 5.

TORTILLAS VENEZOLANAS

Corn Pancakes

These go well with sour cream but they are good plain too!

1-1/2 cups corn kernels, cut from 2 left over (cooked) corn on the cob (or 1-1/2 cups frozen corn kernels, cooked)
1 cup unbleached white flour
1 tsp baking powder
1-1/2 tsp salt
1/4 tsp pepper
2 eggs
1/3 cup nonfat milk
1 tbsp veg oil
Vegetable oil for frying

Dry corn kernels well with paper towel. Set aside. Sift flour with next three ingredients. Beat eggs, add milk and oil, then flour and beat until smooth. Add dry corn kernels.

In large frying pan, heat oil; in it drop the batter by the tablespoonful, and spread into an even circle. As tortillas begin to set, and bottoms turn a light golden color, turn over and fry to a rich golden color. Frying time, approximately 5 to 6 minutes.

When ready, place tortillas on paper towel to absorb oil, then place them in a warm oven until serving time.

Garnish with watercress or parsley. Makes about 20 medium size tortillas.

Desserts

FLAN DE LECHE CON CARAMELO

Caramel Custard

Peru / a favorite in Latin America

3 cups evaporated skimmed milk
3 cups water
1 cup sugar
1/4 tsp salt
Lemon rind
6 large eggs

Place milk, water, sugar, salt and lemon rind in large pan. Let it all come to a boil. Reduce heat and simmer for 15 more minutes. Strain and cool.

Add slightly beaten eggs to cool milk mixture and mix well. Pour into custard cups which have been coated with caramel.

CARAMELO

Caramel

1 cup sugar
1/4 cup water

In medium size pan, mix sugar and water. Let it come to a boil, without stirring, until it begins to turn a very light golden color. Remove from heat and pour about 1-1/2 teaspoons caramel syrup inside each custard cup.

To a large rectangular aluminum pan, add 2 cups hot water and place custard cups inside this pan. Bake in 400° oven for 1 hr. Place custard cups in refrigerator until well chilled.

Just before serving time, turn custard cups over individual serving plates.

Serves 10.

PANQUEQUES LIVIANOS

Light Pancakes

Very good at breakfast time, Tobago.

2 cups unbleached flour
5 tsp baking powder
1 tsp salt
3 tbsp sugar
2 eggs
2 cups nonfat milk
1/3 cup veg oil

Sift flour with next 3 ingredients. Beat eggs in a large mixing bowl. Add milk and oil, then flour mixture and beat until smooth. In large skillet, heat small amount of vegetable oil, pour out about 1/4 cup batter for each pancake. Fry until under side is a nice golden color, then turn and bake on other side.

Serve with hot maple syrup. Makes 24 pancakes.

FLAN DE FRESAS

Strawberry Flan

Peru / or better known as strawberry Bavarian. Make this dessert in late May or early June when strawberries are so plentiful.

1 qt fresh strawberries
1/2 cup sugar, or more, to taste
1 small envelope of unflavored gelatin
2 tbsp cold water
1-1/2 tsp lemon juice
1 can evaporated skimmed milk (which has been placed, unopened, in freezing compartment of refrigerator for 2 hours)

Wash and hull the berries, saving 6 or 7 strawberries for garnish. Put the rest of berries in blender and add sugar. Blend well.

Place gelatin inside a Pyrex cup and dissolve with cold water. Let it soften 5 minutes. Place this cup over hot water, till gelatin liquid is clear. Add gelatin to strawberry puree, then stir in lemon juice and mix well.

Now, beat the entire contents of can of evaporated skimmed milk until stiff and fold into the strawberry mixture. Turn into a serving bowl. Chill 1 hour.

Garnish with fresh strawberries. Serves 10.

BOLLOS DE CREMA

Cream Puffs

These can be had at the many pastry shops that are so abundant in Lima

1 cup water, boiling
1/2 cup shortening
1 cup flour
3 eggs

Boil water in medium size pan. Add shortening and stir until it melts. Empty the flour into the pan. Stir and cook until thick and grainy in appearance.

Remove and empty into bowl of electric mixer. Add eggs to the cooked paste. Beat well. When paste is smooth, shape into 12 cream puffs by dropping from a spoon on baking sheet.

Bake in 400° oven for 30 minutes. Cut off tops while hot. Cool and fill with cream filling.

Replace tops and sprinkle with confectioners sugar. Makes 12 cream puffs.

RELLENO DE CREMA

Cream Filling

2/3 cup sugar
4 tbsp corn starch
1/4 tsp salt
2 cups milk
2 eggs
1 tbsp margarine
1 tsp vanilla

In medium size pan, blend sugar, corn starch and salt together. Add milk slowly, stirring well. Cook over low heat until thickened. Beat eggs well and pour into cooked filling, stirring constantly. Cook 10 minutes. Stir in margarine and vanilla. Cool before using.

PICARONES

Doughnuts—Peruvian style.

A very nourishing dessert resembling doughnuts, very typical of Peru.

1 pkg dry granular yeast
1/4 cup lukewarm water
1 cup water
1 tsp anisette (optional)
1/2 tsp salt
2 eggs
1 cup cooked, mashed acorn squash
4 cups flour
1 cup yellow corn meal
1 cup veg oil

Crumble granular yeast into 1/4 cup lukewarm water. Let it soften 10 minutes. In a large bowl combine water, anisette, salt. Add yeast mixture and eggs. Stir well. Add mashed squash and mix thoroughly. Add flour, yellow corn meal and 3 tbsp veg oil. Stir well with wooden spoon. Place in clean bowl. Cover with clean cloth and let it rise in warm place until double, about 2 hours.

In large skillet, heat oil; take a little dough in your wet hand and open hand slowly, dropping dough into hot oil, making sure there is an opening left in the center with wooden skewer (it should resemble a doughnut).

Remove "picarones" with the skewer after they have turned a light golden color on both sides. Drain on absorbent paper. Serve with brown syrup.

ALMIBAR
Brown Syrup

2 cups brown sugar
1/2 cup water
Orange peel from one med size orange

Boil sugar, water and orange peel for about 15 minutes. Serve over picarones.

PASTEL DE LIMON
Lime Pie

This pie is made with the true lime of the Tropics. Trinidad.

18 Graham crackers
1/3 cup soft margarine
5 eggs
1 cup condensed milk
1/2 cup freshly squeezed lime juice
3 tbsp confectioners sugar
Pinch of salt

Crush Graham crackers to fine crumbs in blender. Place crumbs in bowl. Add margarine and mix well with fork. Place into 8" Pyrex round glass pan and shape with bottom of heavy glass into a pie shell. Bake at 350° for 6 minutes. Let it cool.

Beat 3 egg yolks well (save extra yolk for hair conditioning). Add condensed milk and lime juice and continue beating for 2 more minutes. Pour into pie shell.

Next beat five egg whites till stiff, add confectioners sugar and pinch of salt, beat till it stands in mounds. Pile beaten egg whites on top of pie and bake for 10 more minutes.

Serves 6.

BIZCOCHO BORRACHO
Trifle

The English in my blood shows right through! This well known English dessert is made with a combination of cream sherry, spongecake, pudding and jam.

Pudding
1/4 cup cornstarch
1/2 tsp salt
1/2 cup sugar
2 cups lowfat milk
1 egg, separated
2 tbsp margarine
1-1/2 tsp vanilla

Blend cornstarch, salt and sugar in a bowl. Stir in 1 cup of the milk until smooth. Heat rest of milk, add the cornstarch mixture, and stir constantly over direct heat until it boils and thickens. Pour this hot mixture over slightly beaten egg yolk and mix well. Fold in stiffly beaten egg white. Stir in margarine and vanilla. Refrigerate until ready to use.

Spongecake

4 eggs
1 cup unbleached sifted flour
1 tsp baking powder
1/4 tsp salt
1/4 tsp cream of tartar
1 cup sugar
1 tsp vanilla extract
1 tsp lemon juice
1 cup sherry
6 tbsp raspberry or strawberry preserves
1/2 cup evaporated skimmed milk, very cold, whipped

Line bottoms of two 8 inch layer cake pans with waxed paper. Grease paper lightly. Preheat oven to 350°, 10 minutes before baking time. Eggs should be at room temperature. Place whites in large mixing bowl, yolks in small bowl. Sift flour, baking powder and salt. Add cream of tartar to egg whites. Beat whites until foamy. Gradually beat in 1/2 cup sugar. Continue beating until stiff.

Beat egg yolks until thick. Gradually beat in remaining sugar. Beat until thick and light. Add vanilla and lemon juice. Blend flour mixture into egg yolk mixture and fold into egg white mixture.

Pour batter into prepared cake pans. Bake 25 to 30 minutes, or until surface springs back when lightly pressed with fingertip.

Invert pans. Cool 1 hour. Loosen around edge. Tap pan to loosen. Makes two 8-inch layers.

Split spongecake layers in half to make four layers in all. Sprinkle each layer with sherry. Spread each of three layers with 2 tablespoons preserve. Stack prepared layers, jam side up, spreading each with pudding. Top with plain layer and pudding. Cover. Refrigerate.

Serve with whipped cream. Serves 10.

ALFAJORES
Filled Cookies

These are delicate sandwich-style filled cookies from Peru which are very popular at all times.

1-1/4 cup flour
1-1/4 cup corn starch
1 tsp baking powder
1/4 tsp salt
3/4 cup confectioners sugar
6 oz margarine
1 large egg
1 tsp vanilla
1 14 oz can condensed milk (unopened) or 1 cup homemade Manjarblanco Gloria, pg. 103

Sift flour, corn starch, baking powder, salt and sugar. Cut in margarine till flour mixture resembles small peas. Mix in egg and vanilla very well.

Ingredients have to be well chilled before rolling dough on floured counter to 1/4-inch thick. Cut with very small glass dipped in flour.

Place small circles on cookie sheet and bake at 300° for about 15 to 20 minutes, or until a very light golden color. About 4 dozen cookies.

Filling

Fill cookies with cold homemade blanc mange (Manjarblanco Gloria) pg. 103 (or place can of condensed milk (unopened) in medium sized pan, cover with water and cook covered for 1-1/2 hours. Cool. (If you are familiar with pressure cookers, this time will be shortened considerably, by placing unopened can of milk in pressure cooker with about 2 cups water.) Cook for 25 minutes and let pressure go down normally.

BUDIN DE PAN
Bread Pudding

Surinam.

5 slices 4 day old bread (whole wheat or white)
2 tbsp margarine
1/2 cup raisins
3 cups nonfat milk
3 eggs
1/4 tsp salt
3/4 cup sugar
1 tsp vanilla
1/4 tsp cinnamon
3 tbsp chopped walnuts (optional)

Butter an 11x7-inch glass baking dish. Start oven 10 minutes before baking. Set to 350°.

Toast bread lightly, then spread with margarine while hot. Cut or break slices in quarters. Fit neatly in prepared dish, overlapping slightly.

Scald milk with raisins. Beat eggs slightly in a large bowl. Stir in salt and all but 2 tablespoons of the sugar, then hot milk, raisins and vanilla.

Pour over toast and let stand 10 minutes, pressing toast down well several times to soak up milk mixture. Blend cinnamon with remaining sugar and sprinkle over top.

Sprinkle chopped walnuts on top if desired. Bake 30 minutes, or until top is golden brown. Serve warm. Serves 6.

GALLETITAS MEDIA LUNA CON ALMENDRAS

Almond Crescents

Favorite at Christmas time—very crunchy, Puerto Rico.

1 cup flour
Pinch salt
1/2 cup margarine
1/3 cup Confectioners sugar
1 tsp vanilla extract
1/2 cup almonds, chopped
Confectioners sugar

Heat oven to 325°. Mix flour with salt. Cream margarine with sugar thoroughly. Stir in vanilla extract, chopped almonds and flour. Knead dough several times. Roll dough into long thin ropes.

Cut ropes into 1-inch lengths, rolling each piece until double in length. Place on baking sheet, curving them into crescent shaped cookies. Bake 15 minutes or until a nice pale golden color. Remove to platter. Cool.

Shake crescents in paper bag with Confectioners sugar. Makes about 1-1/2 dozen.

CREPES SUZETTES

A favorite at our household at all times!

1 cup flour
1-1/2 tsp baking powder
1/2 tsp salt
3 tsp sugar
2 eggs
2 tbsp veg oil
2 cups nonfat milk
1/4 cup hot orange juice

Place first seven ingredients in blender. Blend for 2 minutes or until well blended. Let mix rest in refrigerator for 2 hrs. or longer.

Fry on hot greased frying pan, using about three tablespoons of batter for each crepe. Dip hot crepes in Suzette Sauce and fold.

Arrange in serving plate and pour about 1/4 cup of very hot orange juice over crepes. If desired pour brandy over crepes. Ignite and serve immediately. Serves 6.

ALMIBAR DE NARANJA

Suzette Sauce

1/4 cup margarine
1/2 cup sugar
1 tsp orange rind, grated
1/2 tsp lemon rind, grated
1/4 cup orange juice
1/4 cup Curacao

Place all ingredients in small saucepan. Cook slowly for a few minutes until slightly thickened.

BIZCOCHO PARA FIESTA

Peruvian Fiesta Torte (delicious but not low in cholesterol).
Yellow Cake

Cake with Pineapple Cream Filling and Mocha Frosting.

6 eggs
1 cup sugar
1-1/2 tsp vanilla extract
1 cup sifted flour
1/4 cup vegetable oil

Grease and line two 8-inch cake pans with wax paper and grease paper lightly. Start oven 10 minutes before baking time.

Beat eggs until very foamy, scraping sides of bowl often, about 10 minutes. Add sugar and beat until very creamy, scraping sides and bottom of bowl often. Add vanilla extract. Fold in flour carefully. Add vegetable oil and stir till well mixed with rest of ingredients. Pour batter into prepared pans.

Bake in 350° oven for 25 to 30 minutes. Cool in pans. Peel wax paper off cakes. Cut each cake in half, lengthwise, and fill all layers with pineapple cream filling.

Frost top and sides with mocha frosting and sprinkle with chopped nuts.

Relleno De Piña
Pineapple Cream Filling for Torte

1-1/2 cups heavy cream
4 tbsp Confectioners sugar
1 tbsp pineapple juice
4 tbsp crushed pineapple (canned)

Whip cream until stiff. Mix Confectioners sugar with pineapple juice and pineapple. Blend all ingredients carefully into whipped cream.

Crema Moka
Mocha Frosting for Torte

1-1/2 cups heavy cream
4 tbsp Confectioners sugar
4 tsp cocoa
2 tbsp strong coffee
Chopped nuts

Whip cream until stiff. Mix Confectioners sugar with cocoa and coffee. Sprinkle frosted cake with chopped nuts.

TORTA HELADA DE MELOCOTON
Molded Cold Peach Cake

Picture pretty! Peru.

3 eggs
1/2 cup sugar
1 tsp vanilla extract
1/2 cup flour
1/4 stick melted margarine

Break eggs into bowl of electric mixer. Beat eggs until foamy. Beat in sugar and beat at high speed for 2 minutes. Beat in vanilla extract. Fold in flour, using rubber spatula. Cool melted margarine and fold in carefully.

Grease bottom of 8-inch cake pan (or frying pan) line with wax paper and grease paper lightly. Pour batter into prepared cake pan.

Bake in 350° oven for 30 minutes. Remove cake from pan immediately, strip off paper and cool cake.

RELLENO

Filling for Molded Cold Peach Cake.

1 6 oz orange gelatin dessert
1 envelope, Knox plain gelatin
3 cups boiling water
1 cup peach juice
1 lb sliced peaches
1 cup evaporated skimmed milk (very cold)
1/2 cup Confectioners sugar
1/3 cup Curacao
1 tbsp peach juice

Dissolve gelatin in boiling water thoroughly. Add 1 cup peach juice. Pour one cup of this mixture in 10-inch cake pan (or frying pan) which has been greased. Let it set in refrigerator. Place sliced peaches all around set gelatine. Pour another cup of gelatine on top of peaches, let it set again.

Beat evaporated milk with Confectioners sugar till fluffy. Add rest of gelatine mix, blend well. Pour some on top of set peaches. Cut cake into two layers and pour Curacao plus 1 tablespoon peach juice on both layers. Place one layer on top of set gelatin. Pour 1/3 more gelatin mix on top. Place second layer over this and pour remaining gelatin mix over whole cake and sides. Smooth all around.

Place in refrigerator to set for 2 hours. Loosen edge with spatula and turn over on cake platter and serve. Serves 20.

PANQUEQUES DE AVENA Y PLATANO

Banana Oatmeal Pancakes

We ate lots of these pancakes while vacationing near Cuba.

1-1/2 cups quick-cooking oats
2 cups nonfat milk
1/2 tsp salt
1 tbsp honey
1/4 cup veg. oil
2 mashed ripe bananas
2 eggs
1/3 cup unbleached flour
2 tsp baking powder
1/4 tsp cinnamon

Place first four ingredients in medium size pan. Let it come to a slow boil. Turn heat off. Cover and let it cool a few minutes. Add vegetable oil, mashed bananas, two egg yolks and mix well. Sift in flour with baking powder and cinnamon. Add to oatmeal mixture. Beat two egg whites until stiff. Fold into oatmeal mixture.

Heat frying pan; add about a teaspoon vegetable oil to coat the surface. Pour about 1/3 cup oatmeal mixture onto hot frying pan for each pancake, spreading it out with a spoon so it will fry evenly. Fry over medium heat till pancakes are a golden brown.

Serve warm with either Maple syrup or sprinkled with sugar. Serves 6.

MERENGUES

Meringues

Peru / with orange-cream filling. These are served at many tea parties and are a favorite of my childhood days.

6 egg whites
2 cups sugar
1 tsp white vinegar
2 tsp vanilla extract

Put two layers of wax paper on baking sheet. Set oven at 250°. Beat egg whites until they form pointed peaks. Add sugar in small portions and beat well after each addition. Add vinegar and vanilla. Blend in well.

Drop mixture by teaspoonfuls onto prepared sheet. Bake 30 minutes or until a pale white color.

Remove from paper and place on platter. Spread bottom of one meringue with filling and place another one on top, in sandwich fashion. Makes about 36 filled meringues.

RELLENO DE CREMA DE NARANJA

Orange Cream Filling for Meringues

4 tbsp soft margarine
2/3 cup Confectioners sugar
2 tsp orange juice

Mix soft margarine with Confectioners sugar. Add orange juice, creaming well till very smooth.

PLATANOS ACARAMELADOS, ESTILO CHINO

Caramel Bananas

We tried this dessert of Santa Lucia for the first time, and loved it!

1 cup flour
1-1/2 cups water
1 tsp baking powder
1 tsp sugar
3 large bananas
2 cups veg oil
1-1/3 cups sugar
1/3 cup water

Mix flour, water, baking powder and 1 teaspoon sugar well. Peel bananas and slice in 1 inch pieces. Dip banana pieces in batter.

In heavy pan, heat oil; in it fry each banana slice to a light golden color. Make caramel syrup now by mixing 1-1/3 cup sugar with water in heavy pan. Turn heat on. Let it come to a boil without stirring until syrup spins a 5" thread.

Next, lower each banana fritter in hot caramel syrup. Lift carefully and place each one on greased platter. Serves 5. Try this with apples also.

TURRON DE DOÑA PEPA

Doña Pepas Lattice Pastry

Peru / This is the colorful and famous pastry made in Lima every October for the religious celebration of the "Feast of El Señor De Los Milagros" (The Lord of Miracles.)

6 cups flour
3 cups shortening
1 cup cold water mixed with
1/2 tsp yellow coloring and
3 tsp salt
Colored candy (confetti decorator sugar)

Sift flour and place in deep bowl. Add shortening and cut it in with two knives till flour resembles the size of peas. Add water. Mix well and shape dough into narrow cigar shaped sticks about 6-inches long.

Bake sticks on aluminum cookie sheet in 325° oven, for 30 minutes or until sticks are golden in color.

Dip sticks in hot syrup placing one layer of 6 sticks on wax paper. Now place a second layer on top, crosswise. You will have enough sticks to make about 5 7-inch cake sized "turrones." Decorate with colored candy.

ALMIBAR PARA EL TURRON

Syrup for Turron

6 cups sugar
1 cup packed brown sugar
2 cups water
1 cinnamon stick
Juice of 1 orange, and peeling of 1 orange
Juice of 1 lime

In heavy deep pan, put both white and brown sugar with 2 cups water, cinnamon stick, orange peel, orange juice. Let it all come to a boil. Add lime juice. Cook without stirring, to soft ball stage. Dip sticks in this syrup immediately.

ARROZ CON LECHE

Rice Pudding

Peru / and so good!

1 cup enriched long grain rice
4 cups warm water
1 13 oz. evaporated skimmed milk
1 14 oz can condensed milk
Ground cinnamon

Place rice and water in large pan. Cover and boil over medium heat for 20 minutes or until rice is tender. Add next two ingredients and stir well. Let it come to a boil. Lower heat and simmer for about 20 minutes, stirring constantly with wooden spoon.

Garnish with ground cinnamon. Serves 6.

FRIJOLES COLADOS

Sweet Beans

Peru / This is not only delicious, but provides lots of protein and vitamin B as well! A very typical dessert from Peru.

1 lb red kidney beans—lots of water
2 cups water
3 cups evaporated skimmed milk
3 cups sugar
1/2 cup water
1 tsp clove powder
Sesame seeds, roasted

Place beans in very large container and cover with lots of water. Soak beans overnight.

Next day, drain and cook in pressure cooker with 2 cups water for 30 minutes. Let pressure go down normally.

Drain beans and put in blender with milk. Blend well. In separate heavy pan, place sugar, half cup water, clove powder, and cook to the soft ball stage, without stirring. Add blended beans and cook stirring frequently with wooden spoon until you see bottom of pan.

When ready, pour into serving bowl and sprinkle with Sesame seeds. (These have been browned quickly in hot frying pan). Serves 15 to 20 small portions.

MANJARBLANCO GLORIA

Blanc Mange Gloria

Peru / Very good for filling cookies.

1 can evaporated skimmed milk
4 cups low fat milk
2 cups sugar
1 cinnamon stick

Place all ingredients in heavy deep pan. Mix well. Cook over medium heat until liquid begins to thicken. Stir with wooden spoon to prevent scorching. Let it cool and use in your favorite recipes.

ENSALADA DE FRUTA DEL CARIBE

Caribbean Fruit Salad

In Costa Rica, as well as in all of Central America, tropical fruit is plentiful. Papayas come in very large sizes, sometimes 16 inches long.

1 small ripe papaya
2 ripe bananas, peeled, diced
2 oranges, peeled and sliced
 in small sections
2 apples, peeled, chopped fine
Juice of 1 lemon
3 tsp sugar

Peel papaya and dispose of seeds. Cut in small cubes. Place in large bowl with rest of ingredients. Mix well. Serves 6.

BIZCOCHO DE ZANAHORIA LYNNE

Lynne's Carrot Cake

This is my daughter's favorite recipe and nutritious too!

1 cup whole wheat flour
1/2 cup soy flour
2 tsp cinnamon
2 tsp soda
1/2 tsp salt
3 eggs, slightly beaten
3/4 cup veg oil
3/4 cup buttermilk
1-1/2 cups brown sugar
2 cups grated carrots
1 cup crushed pineapple
 (drained)
1/4 cup walnuts, chopped
1/2 cup wheat germ
2 ripe bananas, mashed

Mix all ingredients, blending well. Bake in a greased tube pan or rectangular pan in a 350° oven for 1 hour. Let it cool completely before placing on serving platter. Spread with cream cheese frosting.

Cream Cheese Frosting (a wonderful but not low fat topping)

1 8 oz package cream cheese
1 tbsp margarine
1 tsp vanilla
1 cup Confectioners sugar

Beat cream cheese with margarine until fluffy. Add vanilla and Confectioners sugar gradually until well blended. Spread on cake.

Beverages

CHICHA MORADA

Purple Corn Drink

Peru / Well known drink and healthy too!

4 ears dry purple corn*
1-1/2 gallons water
1-1/2 cups dark brown sugar, or to taste
1 cinnamon stick
1 tsp cloves
skin of 1 pineapple
3 limes

Place purple corn in large pot, with water and next four ingredients. Let it come to a boil. Cover and simmer for 30 minutes.

When lukewarm, strain into a large pitcher. Add the juice of 3 limes. Serve cold.

* Purple corn can be bought at local markets around Halloween time. Choose those with a deep purple color.

CAFE EXPRESO

Brazil / This coffee will keep you alert all day!

6 tbsp drip grind coffee
7 demi-tasse cups of water
Cheesecloth or 2 sheets of Towel paper

Put water in pan and let it come to a boil. Add coffee and as soon as it comes to a boil, turn heat off and pour coffee through cheesecloth or through 2 sheets of towel paper, which have been placed inside a strainer and strain coffee into a coffee pot.

Serve hot. Serves 6.

BATIDA DE CAFE CON LECHE

Cafe Au Lait

Particularly good on a cold winter night.

3 cups very strong hot coffee
3 cups low fat milk, scalded
6 tsp sugar (or to taste)

Place all ingredients in the blender. Blend for 1/2 a minute. Serve hot. Serves 6.

Glossary

Anise	Aromatic seed of licoricelike flavor in powdered form may be used to season "picarones."
Basil	Aromatic herb, leaves of which are used in Italian food, stews, tomato, and cheese dishes.
Bay Leaf	For use in Italian and Latin dishes.
Blend	To carefully mix different ingredients.
Caramel	Sugar which has been browned by heating.
Cassava	(Also known as yuca or aipim) a starchy tropical plant which can be purchased at Latin markets. It's better to buy the frozen yuca, as it will keep very well, whereas the fresh yuca needs to be cooked right away.
Chili pepper	For use in dishes requiring a very hot seasoning.
Chopped	Cut up a food into medium size pieces.
Cornhusks	When you buy fresh corn, save the cornhusks. These will keep for a very long time. Or, you can also buy them at Latin markets. Cornhusks can be used as a replacement for aluminum foil in cooking.
Crepe	A thin French pancake.
Crouton	Slices of bread, toasted, buttered, and cut into small cubes.
Culantro	(Chinese parsley) used in many Peruvian dishes and can be found in Latin as well as Chinese markets.
Cumin	An aromatic seed in powder form, used to season meat.
Curry	A powdered preparation of spices used to season Indian dishes and eggs.
Dice	To cut into very small cubes.
Filet	A strip of meat without bones.
Fillet	A strip of fish without bones.
Garlic	Use fresh cloves of garlic whenever possible. Used in Latin and many Italian dishes.

Ginger	Buy it by the root—for use in Oriental dishes.
Fold	To blend a mixture very gently into another mixture.
Garnish	Food used to decorate and to improve the flavor of a dish.
Marinade	A well seasoned liquid in which food is immersed for a length of time.
Mince	To cut into tiny pieces.
Mung Beans	May be purchased at Chinese markets and used to grow bean sprouts.
Oregano	Use on lentils, spaghetti, salads, lamb, poultry, broccoli.
Paprika	A kind of powdered red pepper, but not too strong to taste.
Parsley	Used in many Latin dishes and also as a garnish.
Purple Corn	Can be bought at local markets around Halloween time—choose those with a deep purple color.
Saute	To cook food over moderate heat in a small amount of vegetable oil.
Simmer	To slowly cook food at a very low temperature.
Soft Ball Stage	Drop hot sugar mixture into a small dish filled with cold water. Roll mixture into a small ball. If it holds its shape it has reached the "soft ball stage."
Thyme	Aromatic herb leaves used in chowders, cheese dishes, stuffings, meats and sauces for meats.

ABBREVIATIONS

lbs—pounds
tbsp—tablespoon
tsp—teaspoon
veg—vegetable
oz—ounce
med—medium
gran—granulated

Index

SEAFOOD

MEAT COOKERY